Sex, alcohol and other drugs
Exploring the links in young people's lives

Jeanie Lynch and Simon Blake

National Children's Bureau

The National Children's Bureau promotes the interests and well-being of all children and young people across every aspect of their lives. NCB advocates the participation of children and young people in all matters affecting them. NCB challenges disadvantage in childhood.

Sex Education Forum

The Sex Education Forum is the national authority on sex and relationships education. The Forum was established in 1987 and is based at the National Children's Bureau. It is an umbrella body bringing together over 50 national organisations involved in sex and relationships education. Member organisations work together to share good practice, and to articulate a common voice in support of sex and relationships education for all children and young people.

Drug Education Forum

The Drug Education Forum brings together a range of national organisations from health, education, police and voluntary sectors that support the delivery of drug education. The Forum promotes the provision of effective drug education for all children and young people. The Drug Education Forum believes that the purpose of drug education is to increase children's and young people's knowledge and understanding of drugs and their usage, and help them develop skills and attitudes, so that they can make informed choices.

Published by the National Children's Bureau, 8 Wakley Street, London EC1V 7QE. Tel: 020 7843 6000. Website: www.ncb.org.uk
Registered Charity number 258825

ISBN 1 904787 09 6

British Library Cataloguing in Publication Data
A catalogue record for this book is available from the British Library

Contents

About the authors

Jeanie Lynch is Project Development Officer, Children's Development at NCB. She has worked for a number of years on sexual health promotion and sex and relationships education for vulnerable or marginalised groups of children and young people, particularly those who are in care, homeless or at risk of sexual exploitation.

Simon Blake is Assistant Director of Children's Development. He is the lead for PSHE and Citizenship in education settings and a former Director of the Sex Education Forum. He is a member of the Teenage Pregnancy Unit Independent Advisory Group.

Acknowledgements

Many people have generously contributed to this resource. The voice of young people was crucial and central to its development, so thank you to all who gave us their views, and for helping us to make the links, clarify the issues and explore ways forward. Particular thanks to:

Ollie Entwhistle   David Morris   Hawa Osman
Sarah Roberts   Kieri Sutton   Lorna Webley
Natalie Young

Thank you also to the adults who took part, speaking honestly about the issues, opportunities and dilemmas they faced when talking to young people about the links between sex, alcohol and other drugs. There are too many of you to name individually, but we hope that we have managed to capture your views and perspectives. The following people have all made particularly generous contributions to the development of this resource:

Jo Adams   Tony Atkin   Michelle Barry
Max Biddulph   Celia Bowden   Adrian Bowden-Green
Rob Brown   Angie Brown-Simpson   David Clarke
Lester Coleman   Steve Dorney   Mark Dunn
Simeon Earnshaw   Kim Jewel Elliot   Gill Frances
Louisa Hoey   Joan Hughes   Helen Humphries
Roger Ingham   Dot Kesterton   Adrian King

Rob Kurn	Helen Lee	Trefor Lloyd
Paul Matthews	Peter Matthews	Rachel Monaghan
Stella Muttock	Siobhan McFeely	Christine McInnes
Karin O'Sullivan	Anne Shutt	Nicola Sinclair
Denise Wheatman	Pam Wilson	

Thanks as ever to Tracey Anderson for consistently brilliant administration.

Finally thank you to the Department of Health for funding the Sex, Alcohol and Other Drugs Project and this resource.

Foreword

In August I travelled down from Buxton to London for three Saturdays to help out with 'Sex and drugs – the links explored' (SADLE).

I met up with other young people from Wakefield, Southampton and London, and together we discussed what we thought were the most important issues. We agreed that young people who are drunk or who have taken drugs are more likely to take sexual risks. Many of us felt that schools don't address this issue properly. We are taught about drugs and sexual health, but teachers rarely mention the links between the two. I'd like to see these subjects taught together rather than separately.

Natalie Young – Buxton for Youth Project

We feel young people do not get enough relevant education about sex and related issues and it is important that young people learn about the risks involved. As we now know from our research for the SADLE project, and from talking to our peers, many young people put themselves at risk when under the influence of alcohol or drugs by having unprotected sex. They need to learn how to reduce this risk and keep themselves safe. We all enjoyed being part of the SADLE project and it was great to meet other young people and share ideas.

It let us learn about other issues facing young people, and think about how we put ourselves at risk sometimes without realising.

Kieri Sutton, Lorna Webley and David Morris – Wakefield Peer Education Project

The relationship between sex, alcohol and other drugs is a complex one. We do need to learn much more about the ways in which young people are socialised into alcohol and drug use, the role drugs play in enabling and/or inhibiting social and sexual activities, activities supporting or harming reputations, and so on. But meanwhile, the issues need to be addressed together with young people.

This resource is based firmly on two principles. First, that we should no longer regard risk domains as separate but begin to explore how they can be related and considered together. Second, the ideas are based on wide consultations with young people themselves.
It does not encourage 'preaching', it accepts that young people are vulnerable and subject to pressures of one kind or another, and it recognises the willingness of young people to contribute towards finding ways through their complex social worlds in a way that will minimise harm and damage.

I am sure that this resource will be extremely useful to those engaged with young people in schools, youth work, health, care and other settings, to work constructively with young people and to support them in achieving a good balance between enjoyment and responsibility to themselves and others.

Dr Roger Ingham, Director, Centre for Sexual Health Research, University of Southampton and Member of the Teenage Pregnancy Unit Independent Advisory Group

Why this resource, who is it for and how to use it?

Sex, alcohol and other drugs is the result of a two-year project, which set out to explore and understand the links between sex, alcohol and other drugs. We wanted to develop understanding of how professionals in a range of settings can help all young people including those with disabilities to understand the links and develop the skills, confidence and beliefs that help them to manage risks. The project has been both exciting and challenging. The links between sex, alcohol and other drugs are acknowledged in strategies and guidance such as the *Teenage Pregnancy* Report (Social Exclusion Unit 1999), *Drugs: Guidance for Schools Consultation Document* (DfES 2003) and *Alcohol and Teenage Pregnancy* Briefing (Alcohol Concern 2002). However, although the links are recognised, both national and local policy and understanding of best practice is underdeveloped.

Through the project we came to understand that for some young people as for many adults there may be potential benefits as well as risks in using alcohol and other drugs in sex and relationships. It also encouraged us to think about the continued separation between sex and relationships, alcohol and other drugs in education and health and challenged us to develop creative approaches in education and health that reflect the 'joined-upness' of young people's lives.

There is no one apparent reason why some young people use alcohol and other drugs as part of their sexual development and relationships. It is a combination of our prevailing culture, sexual exploration, vulnerability, nervousness, personality, excitement and opportunity or lack of it.

We knew this work would challenge us, both personally and professionally, as well as challenge much current policy and practice. We learnt very quickly that professionals need support and confidence, and a robust policy framework alongside professional development to effectively explore the links between sex, alcohol and other drugs with young people. At the end of this piece of work we are even more convinced of its importance than we were at the start.

Who is it for?

This resource has been written to respond to the expressed needs of those we consulted and will therefore be useful for:

- teachers in secondary schools, pupil referral units and further education colleges
- Connexions personal advisors and learning mentors
- local healthy school workers
- teenage pregnancy workers
- drug action team workers
- youth workers
- school and community nurses
- public health specialists
- residential social workers
- outreach workers
- sexual health, drug and alcohol, and one-stop service staff.

How was it developed?

This resource was developed from:

- a review of the literature
- a mapping exercise of existing practice

- consultation with teachers, youth and community workers, social care, health professionals and sexual health and drug specialists
- an expert working seminar
- a peer-led 'research' process in which eight young people developed a questionnaire and interviewed their peers
- consultation with young people in focus group settings
- developmental work in schools and youth settings and focus group evaluation of this work.

The project was guided by an advisory group who helped to think through the issues, clarify the implications and advise us on practical approaches.

About the resource and how to use it

Sex, alcohol and other drugs is one of three resources which address the links between sex, alcohol and other drugs funded by the Department of Health since the Teenage Pregnancy Strategy was published in 1999.

- Alcohol Concern and DrugScope have produced a briefing paper, *Alcohol and Teenage Pregnancy*. This paper examines the evidence of the links between alcohol and teenage pregnancy.
- Tacade have produced a resource pack, *Sex, Drugs and Alcohol,* with clear, practical activities for addressing the issues with young people.

These resources have been developed to complement each other. The key aim of *Sex, alcohol and other drugs* is to explore and clarify the issues, drawing heavily on the perspectives of young people, professionals and research, and to explore the implications and offer practical ideas for working with young people. It is offered as a starting point for an underdeveloped area of policy and practice.

It is divided into six sections:

Section One draws on the evidence from research and practice. It integrates the learning from the participation work led by young people, the consultations with young people and professionals, as well as the findings from research. This section will be particularly useful for practitioners, policy-makers and strategic planners.

Section Two explores the education and support that young people said they need about sex, alcohol and other drugs, as well as clarifying the issues raised by professionals.

Section Three explores the complexity of the links and implications for policy and practice. It aims to provide a starting point for further development and dialogue between national and local policy-makers and practitioners.

Section Four offers practical suggestions for addressing the issues with young people. It provides a series of case studies and practical ideas. This section will be useful for practitioners wanting to develop the work across different settings.

Section Five addresses continuing professional development.

Section Six provides details of some useful resources and further reading, followed by a list of useful organisations.

Section One
Why is it important to explore the links between sex, alcohol and other drugs?

This section draws on the evidence from research and practice. It integrates the learning from the participation work led by young people, the consultations with young people and professionals, as well as the findings from research. This section will be particularly useful for practitioners, policy-makers and strategic planners.

The link between drug use and sexual behaviour became a key concern for research and interventions during the 1980s with the advent of HIV/AIDS particularly among intravenous drug users (Henderson 2002). The specific culture and context of alcohol and other drug use among young people changes over time and evidence of binge drinking, cocaine and poly drug use, as well as evidence from research and practice of clear links between sex, pregnancy, sexually transmitted infections, alcohol and other drugs make it imperative that young people receive education and support.

'It [sex and drug education] all needs a good rethink. It has got to help us learn about things so we know about them in advance of when they are happening. It is no good waking up and finding you had sex 'cos you were really drunk and not knowing it happens!'
Young man, aged 17

From our work and research (McGrellis *et al.* 2000) with children and young people, we know that they do not think about drugs or sex in a vacuum but relate these to other issues and concerns in their lives. Young people who are given opportunities to discuss and explore the links between sex, alcohol and other drugs openly and honestly are effectively prepared for situations that they might encounter before they happen.

'I think that it would be a good idea to link alcohol, drug and sex education because of the fact that drugs and alcohol have even worse effects when taken together, and maybe, if the person tempted to mix different drugs and alcohol knew about the consequences of their actions, or the side effects, then they might think twice before doing it. Drugs and alcohol can lead to the taker being temporarily unaware to what is going on around him or her, and then the risk of them having unprotected sex is much higher, therefore the risk of infection or an unwanted child gets higher too. Young people especially need to be more aware of the effects and consequences because they are younger and therefore more liable to have advantage taken of them, and they are more impressionable.'
Young man, aged 15

what young people say

'If the teaching involves not only the effects, but the ways to deal with the situation, then the person will know more about what to do in a situation involving drugs, sex and alcohol.'
Young woman, aged 14

There are five national outcomes for children outlined in the green paper *Every Child Matters* (DfES 2003b).

These are:

- **being healthy:** enjoying good physical and mental health and living a healthy lifestyle
- **staying safe:** being protected from harm and neglect and growing up able to look after themselves
- **enjoying and achieving:** getting the most out of life and developing broad skills for adulthood
- **making a positive contribution:** to the community and to society and not engaging in antisocial or offending behaviour
- **economic well-being:** overcoming socio-economic disadvantages to achieve their full potential in life.

Work on the links between sex, alcohol and other drugs contributes to achieving these objectives.

Education and support needs to be informed by the explicit needs of children and young people. This can be achieved by identifying ways of finding out the realities and contexts of young people's lives. The next part of this section draws on a review of literature and our consultations with professionals and young people in a range of settings. It offers:

■ some facts about young people, sex, alcohol and other drugs
■ an analysis of some of the emerging issues.

This provides a starting point from which professionals can involve young people in understanding local trends and issues, and develop effective responses.

What does the evidence from young people and research tell us about young people, sex, alcohol and other drugs?

Some facts

■ In an increasingly consumerist world with easy access to alcohol the risks that young people are willing to take are increasing. Excessive drinking affects judgements and can remove inhibitions. This can lead to unsafe situations such as walking home alone at night, dangerous driving, unsafe sex and consequent unplanned pregnancy and sexually transmitted infections (Alcohol Concern 2002).

■ Young people are having sex earlier, and many are having unsafe and unprotected sex. Alcohol and drug use is often associated with first sexual intercourse among young people, and this can lead to regret (MacHale and Newell 1997, Ingham 2001).

■ Forty per cent of sexually active 13- and 14-year-olds in the UK were 'drunk or stoned' at first intercourse (Wight et al. 2000).

■ Nearly 50 per cent of 15-year-olds have tried drugs and one in five is a regular user. Ten thousand pupils aged between 11 and 15 in 321 schools were surveyed. The prevalence of drug use increased sharply with age – only 6 per cent of 11-year-olds had used drugs in the last year compared with two-fifths (36 per cent) of 15-year-olds. Cannabis was the most frequently reported illegal drug used in the last year, used by 13 per cent. One per cent had used heroin in the last year and 1 per cent had used cocaine. In total, 4 per cent had used Class A drugs in the last yea (DoH 2003).

■ Alcohol and drug use among young people in the UK is greater than in other European countries (Coleman 2001). Surveys suggest that alcohol consumption is on the increase, although the equivalent evidence for drug use is less certain. Young people are drinking more alcohol on a weekly basis. In England, between 1988 and 1999 the numbers of young people aged between 11 and 15 who reported drinking stayed stable at around 21 to 27 pert cent. These figures rose sharply in 1999 with almost half of young people aged 15 reporting that they had drunk alcohol within the last week (DoH 2001).

■ Among 15- to 16-year-olds in Europe, one in 14 had unprotected sex after drinking; among 17-year-olds this rose to one in seven (Hibell et al. 2001).

■ A third of females and almost 40 per cent of males aged 15 and 16 have tried illegal drugs (Plant and Miller 2000).

■ A survey by the Joseph Rowntree Foundation (see Beinhart et al. 2002) reports that, of young people interviewed, more than four out of 10 students in Year 10, and more than half of Year 11, reported drinking more than five units of alcohol in one session – so called 'binge drinking' – with more than a quarter reporting three or more alcohol 'binges' within the previous month.

■ One American study (Hingson et al. 1990) showed that condoms were less likely to be used when alcohol had been consumed. In the same study, the relationship between condom use and drugs was even more significant. Of the young people who had reported intercourse after drinking 16 per cent also reported less condom use on these occasions. In addition, 25 per cent of those who had used drugs before having intercourse reported lower condom use on those occasions.

■ In the National Survey of Sexual Attitudes and Lifestyles study (Wellings *et al.* 1994), almost two-thirds of those who named alcohol as the main contributory factor for first sex also reported using no contraception.

what young people and practitioners say

'It brings us back to what is wrong with our entire culture around sex – this need to get half-drunk beforehand … why does someone have to drink a bottle of cider before going out to meet someone – what message have we given them about sex?'
Outreach worker

'They sometimes wake up feeling dirty because they don't know what they've done the night before.'
Young person

'I woke up with her the next morning, couldn't remember a thing – my first time and I couldn't remember! It was probably the most meaningless thing I have ever done when it was meant to be one of the most special things in my life.'
Young person

Exploring the issues

The issues described here emerged in our work with young people and professionals throughout the SADLE project.

Culture

In Britain, sex and sexuality are not easily discussed. Children and young people learn about sex from a range of sources. Many of them often inaccurate and misleading. Unlike some of our European neighbours, such as Scandinavia and the Netherlands, we do not encourage children and young people to value sex, nor do we emphasise the importance of pleasure and mutuality within relationships. As a result, those working with young people tell us that many young people have sex because it was available, because they were drunk and because they wanted to feel good about themselves (Adams 1997). Given the silence around sex and the potential confidence-boosting effect of alcohol and other drugs, many young people use them to overcome nervousness, embarrassment and vulnerability (Ingham 2001). This is true for many young people who manage and take risks for different reasons. For example, the 'sensation seeker' may be excited and thrilled by the 'naughtiness' of sex so may use alcohol and other drugs to increase the thrill. Others may use alcohol and other drugs to give them the courage to participate in social and sexual situations.

At the same time, alcohol is used in the adult world as a rite of passage, to celebrate, to commiserate, to party, to build confidence and as a way of relaxing at the end of the day. Young people learn very early on that alcohol is an accepted and acceptable drug that is used to excess by many adults on a whole range of occasions – and not least to overcome stress or nervousness. Many are 'inducted' into alcohol use at family occasions well below the legal drinking age. In comparison most other drugs are generally seen as unacceptable. Some children and young people live in homes where violence is a norm and is often linked to parent's alcohol misuse. This has an obvious impact on their emotional health and well-being and their sense of safety.

Young people have diverse family backgrounds that influence their decisions and choices. These may be based on cultural beliefs, life experiences and local traditions. For example, some communities smoke marijuana as part of their cultural tradition and some communities are traditionally 'heavy drinkers'.

The nature of adolescence and transitions to adulthood are changing. The path used to be getting a job, leaving home, and then starting a sexual relationship and marriage. The path has shifted to become having sex, moving out of home and then working (Nielsen and Rudberg 2000). Not only has there been this significant cultural shift, people drink alcohol more and alcohol often plays a major part in these transitions.

Young people reported that the media has a big influence on everyday cultures. Alcohol and other drugs are high profile in everyday media. Many soap operas feature the pub as a central location as well as telling detailed stories of alcohol and sexual activity. 'Reality shows' normalise sex, alcohol and other drugs and there is an increasing gaze on celebrities in magazines. Everyday stories of celebrity separation and divorce with accompanying drug and alcohol use serve to create and maintain a culture that offers mixed messages to young people. Similarly the concerted efforts of alcohol advertisers to target young people supports a culture that both normalises and condones alcohol use yet condemns young people's experimentation and sexual risk-taking.

Some young people tell us that they are motivated to use alcohol and other drugs because it is part of youth culture. Anecdotal and

what young people say

'Me and me mates go into cafés during the day and you can just get a coffee or a lemonade and chill out and chat – there's nothing like that open in the evenings unless it's a youth club and some of us don't want that. So no wonder they end up in pubs, get the beer goggles on, and then get off with each other.'
Young woman, aged 18

'I'd try and make more places for people to go during the day and at night-time. If they've got nowhere really to go, that's why they turn to drugs and alcohol because there's nothing else to do but sit on the road and smoke and drink. If we had places to go then it would be different'.
Young woman, aged 16

biographical evidence shows this was always the case. The specific contexts of young people's lives and the opportunities open to them has an impact on how they 'consume' sex, alcohol and other drugs. Some young people told us that sex, alcohol and other drugs become entertainment, 'there is nothing else to do'.

One group of young people in a rural village described Friday nights as being about 'getting hammered and then snogging and shagging whoever was around'.

Henderson (2002) emphasises the changing nature of alcohol and other drug use as part of the clubbing culture. A decade ago young people in the clubbing context used less alcohol and ecstasy was the drug of choice.

She has also identified the impact of ecstasy and dance culture on gender relations.

> Many girls in 1996 still refer to the lack of 'copping off' pressure as a major part of the enjoyment they get out of the dance party scene. But as the culture has diversified, mutated and regenerated over the years, it has become more sexed up. Invading 'beer monsters' used to think they were on to a good thing with girl 'ravers' and found they got short shrift. The return of alcohol and the rise of cocaine in the culture seem to have accompanied a more gritty return to the 'flesh'. (Henderson 1997)

One young man (aged 19) talked to us about his experience of intimacy with another man while taking ecstasy:

He (a friend) just kept touching my shoulder and hands and saying it's really great to be out with you and looking me right in the eye, but it wasn't a problem – it was quite nice because blokes wouldn't normally do that or they'd get a kicking.

Henderson argues that many traditional stereotypes are broken down when the lights are low and people are using ecstasy and other illegal drugs. Heterosexual men hugging men, women and men massaging each other, dancing in mixed gay and straight groups. And she argues that having experienced this, it is difficult to 'go back', hence the dance culture has a lasting impact on gender relations. More recently alcohol has come 'back on the scene'.

Professionals need to be aware of contemporary local youth cultures to help ensure that education and support responds to the local issues and concerns of young people and policy-makers. Youth culture changes and evolves and is different in different local contexts. This must be understood and addressed in local practice.

As a culture we are not good at making and encouraging learning from mistakes. Often people want to blame or criticise. While we continue to perpetuate this culture it is likely that young people will explain some sexual risk-taking as being a result of alcohol and other drugs when it may be a result of vulnerability, excitement or lack of knowledge. Young people say that alcohol (particularly) and other drugs reduce the sense of self-control (Rhodes and Quirk 1996). Based on interviews with young people, Ingham (2001) suggests that alcohol may be used to explain sexual activity that is regretted and which young people feel ashamed or embarrassed about. So, for example, young people may tell a nurse or doctor that they were drunk when accessing emergency contraception or going for a sexually transmitted infection check-up or may try to ease the guilt and shame for themselves – 'I don't know what happened, I was really drunk'.

Some young people described going further than they anticipated or making a mistake that they would regret later. One young woman (aged 18) talked about cheating on her boyfriend with his best mate, 'both dumped me afterwards and told everyone I was a right slag'.

Many young people expressed a dissonance between what they hoped for themselves and the actual realities of their lives. Clearly all education and support must play a role in supporting young people to develop their own moral framework to guide their behaviours as well as help them manage and recover from mistakes. Many also express regret at the realities and how they do not match their hopes and dreams. One young woman, aged 17, talking about her first sexual intercourse, stated:

> I regretted it, I really did. I thought, oh God, this is not the way to lose it
> … you're supposed to lose it in a meaningful relationship, you know.
> You're supposed to do it after you have known the guy five or six months,
> you know. There's me on my one night stand, pissed as hell, and lose it in
> someone else's bedroom, you know. I thought, great, well done!
> (Ingham et al 1991)

'There were an awful lot of talks about teenage pregnancies and how important it is to be safe but they seem to cloud over the fact that if you drink or you use drugs your inhibitions go down and therefore it's more risky. People are less likely to be safe and more vulnerable to sexually transmitted infections and things like that.'
Young man, aged 16

'Some people get more emotional.'
Young woman, age 17

'Some go depressed, some laugh a lot, some act weird or aggressive.'
Young man, age 15

Self-discovery, exploration and risk

Growing up is a time of developing independence, self-discovery, learning, making mistakes and gaining a positive sense of identity. In the 21st century, young people have more leisure time, less parental influence, more disposable income and increased pressure from the media to behave in particular ways (Ingham 2001). Children and young people learn through exploration and trying out different things which can involve taking risks.

Risk-taking is often perceived negatively even though research into children's play emphasises the importance of risk-taking in children's emotional and social development (Ball 2002). Leigh (1999) emphasises that there are both positive and negative aspects of risk. The nature of risk-taking itself changes as societies change (Giddens 1991). Taking risks and testing boundaries is an important part of growing up and we assert that sex, alcohol and other drugs are part of this process. Many young people will 'experiment' with sex, alcohol and other drugs as part of working out what they want and don't want in their interpersonal and sexual relationships. For many risk-taking is a way of finding out who they are and who they want to be as well as part of the process of developing their own boundaries and values. As a consequence they may be able to gain more knowledge and develop new skills as well as a greater sense of their own identity.

Research suggests that some people are sensation-seekers and look for thrills and risks to test their own boundaries. Others steer well clear of risks and like to work within their existing comfort and safety zones. There has been much academic debate about the relationship between different types of risk taken by young people. International research shows that young people who use alcohol and other drugs on a regular basis are more likely to report early sexual intercourse and multiple partners (Santelli *et al.* 1998, Ingham 2001). Some researchers suggest some people are naturally risk-takers. So, for example, some people will have unsafe sex, use alcohol and other drugs and drive fast. Others see risk as a series of discrete behaviours and argue that alcohol and other drugs cause sexual risk-taking.

Whilst the research is not conclusive about whether there are 'risk-takers' or whether alcohol and other drugs encourage sexual 'risk-taking', it is clear we must help young people to explore and understand the type of risk they are willing to take as well as assess their own 'risk ability' and develop effective skills and strategies to manage this. For example, 'sensation-seekers' may use alcohol and other drugs to help them take risks sexually and will need to use a different range of strategies and skills to manage their risks than a 'low-risk' person who may use alcohol and other drugs in different ways, or indeed may not use them at all.

Young people's perceptions of risk are also important. Risks may be in terms of risk to reputations – for example, some young people, especially young men (Lloyd 2002), build a 'masculine' reputation based on risk-taking and sexual prowess; whilst similar risk-taking or sexual behaviour among young women may earn them the reputation of 'slag' or 'easy' (Adams 2002). We need to understand risk within the context of young people's lives and recognise that for them the perceived benefits of using alcohol and other drugs in the context of sex and relationships may outweigh the potential public health risks. This is particularly so if we do not provide education and support that addresses the emotional and physical costs and benefits. As one young person said:

'I was using drugs now and again and my social worker thought it would be good for me to go on an adventure holiday where they would be potholing, abseiling and all this other stuff. I said, "No way, I'm not doing that." It was far more risky than doing a bit of spliff.'

The lives of young people are becoming increasingly stressful with ever increasing numbers of mental health problems, including self-harm. Many of the young people discussed how alcohol and other drugs can help them to relax and feel good about themselves. With the frequency and intensity of alcohol use among young people increasing it is important we help them to think about how to manage all risks, including sexual risks, when using alcohol and other drugs. In addition we need to work on stress reduction techniques and offer them timely and appropriate referral and support regarding their emotional and mental health.

'People just take drugs and alcohol through pressure and stress as well. When people get really stressed they just need something to relax and stuff. We always see adults saying "I need a good old drink".'
Young woman, aged 14

Power and inclusion

Stereotypes, expectations and peer group norms have long been recognised as having a substantial influence on young people's behaviour. Aggleton *et al.* (1998) emphasise the different scripts that boys and girls learn within the context of their culture. Traditionally boys are expected to be high-risk takers who are sexually virile. They report sexual risk-taking is more likely if they have used alcohol or if they feel pressured from peers. Many (wilfully or through expectation) look for the excitement of risk-taking. Risk-taking is one indicator of real manhood (Lloyd 2002). Young men are expected to know all about sex and to want it all the time. In the peer group context there is often incredible pressure to be sexually all-knowing and to want sex (Biddulph and Blake 2001). Given this pressure, many young men use alcohol and other drugs to improve their confidence, for example to help them chat people up, risk rejection or have sex.

Although the gender landscape is changing, young women are still expected not to take risks or be sexually assertive. Sex, alcohol and other drugs is one arena in which traditional gender patterns are challenged and shifting. Increasingly commentators are identifying changes in traditional patterns of gender and sexuality. Groups of young women binge drinking and 'out on the pull' are now familiar in most British towns and cities. Despite this public challenge to traditional norms many of those who work with young women argue girl power has not really arrived. Instead, sex, alcohol and other drugs are used to mask vulnerability and, in fact, large numbers of young women are feeling bad about their bodies, having unsafe sex, regretting the sex they have and punishing themselves for it. Many are still reducing their own expectations in order to 'please the boys' (Adams 2002). As one young woman (15) said,

'Lots of my friends spend their time worrying about boys and what the boys think of them. They sit outside the park drinking alcohol so when the boys stop their cars they have the confidence to speak to them and flirt.'

Some young women also feel vulnerable to pressure to have sex from boys who have been drinking. They may feel intimidated by fear of aggression if they refuse, creating another risk factor in the form of coercive sexual activity (Ingham 2001).

Many of the young people (particularly young women) were worried about having their drinks spiked and about date rape.

'It doesn't take five minutes to put something in your drink, play it nice and then take you back where something could happen.'
Young woman, aged 19

The impact of alcohol and other drugs on sexual risk-taking

Alcohol and other drugs lower inhibitions and affect judgement. This can have both negative and positive effects. It can give a person confidence to have sex which they want but might not happen, or which might be more embarrassing without drugs (Plant, Bagnall and

Forster 1990, Ingham 2001). However, it can also make someone less likely to assess risks accurately, and affect people's competence in negotiating the use of, or using, condoms.

'You might use drugs or alcohol to impress the one you fancy.'
Young man, aged 15

'With friends you can drink to have a good time. Some people may use them if a sexually attractive person offers it to them, so they fit in and be as good as they are.'
Young woman, aged 15

Vulnerability, inequalities and prejudice

Some young people are particularly vulnerable to substance misuse and early sexual activity as a result of life experience such as socio-economic disadvantage, poor experience of public care, low self-esteem, sexual abuse or exploitation and exclusion from school or the youth justice system.

Evidence shows that these groups of young people are more likely to be pregnant earlier (Corlyon and McGuire 1997) and have higher levels of substance misuse (Health Advisory Service, Gilvarry 2001). Alcohol and other drugs are often involved in the process when young people are abused through prostitution (Palmer 2001, Van Meeuwen, Swann *et al.* 1998). Some research suggests young people from lower socio-economic groups are more likely to report taking risks (Coleman 2001).

Although many vulnerable young people appear knowledgeable and confident about sex, alcohol and other drugs, the reality is often quite different. They need additional and probably targeted education and support to help develop self-esteem and respect for self and others.

'I met this bloke when I was 12 – you know what it's like – I really fell in love with him, I really fell for it … I thought he loved me as well but he didn't. The next thing I knew, I had a crack problem and he had me working (sexually) for him. I can look back now and know I was wrong but at the time I believed in him.'
Young pregnant care leaver, aged 16

'Some of the others mentioned things I hadn't considered before, such as the peer pressure involved with both drug-taking and under-age sex. Although they're seen as cool, both of them can harm you in some way, and young people end up doing things that they regret just to impress their mates.'
Young woman, aged 15

'They might not be thinking straight and end up doing things they regret afterwards.'
Young person

'The scene is full of people off their heads on beer, poppers, pills, whiz, everyone seems to want to get mashed off their heads. When I first went on the scene I was really nervous and I just got really pissed. It was the only way I could cope with it.'
Young gay man, aged 17

'When I used to get out of it all the time I felt so bad about myself that I just used to let anyone do anything to me. I would sometimes end up messing around with different lads. "So what", I used to think, "I am rough anyway." Now I know that is not how I want it to be.'
Young woman, aged 17, in treatment for drug misuse

'The night before we got sentenced we went out and got really pissed to make sure we got a shag – it could be the last one for a long time. We didn't think about condoms.'
Young man in a Young Offenders Institution, aged 17

Prejudice and discrimination including racism and homophobia can leave many young people with very low self-esteem and feelings of low self-worth. As a result they may use alcohol and other drugs to help them to cope with this discrimination. Estimates put alcohol and drug usage among gay, lesbian and bisexual communities at about three times the general population and this is attributed at least partially to the impact of prejudice (AXM 2003).

Young people with a learning disability are particularly vulnerable to exploitation. There is evidence that this particular group of young people are more likely to be abused by their family and peers (Brown and Craft 1992). Many young people with a learning disability are taking a number of medicines on a daily basis, often administered by others. In response, many schools, FE colleges and other education providers work hard to ensure that these young people get additional support on sex and relationships. Through concrete and participatory learning experiences they are helped to understand the impact of alcohol and other drugs on choices, consent and sexual decision-making. Further work is needed to understand the specific education and support needs of young people with learning disabilities to help them explore the links between sex, alcohol and other drugs and also to help them understand the differences between medicines, alcohol and other drugs.

Other groups of young people tell us that their education does not meet their needs or address their realities. As one young gay man (aged 19) said of his sex and relationships education, 'I felt very, very abnormal and very, very alone'. Many young gay people go out on the commercial gay scene to try and meet others 'like them' and to work out who they are and to learn about sex because the sex and relationships education they had probably did not address gay sexuality well (Blake 2003). This is complicated because the gay scene has a particular culture, which focuses heavily on bodies, sex, alcohol and other drugs.

Gay young people reported the gay commercial scene as a key place for self-discovery.

'The only way I could think of finding out about sex was to actually find someone and doing it.'
Young man, aged 19

Inadequate education and support contributes to vulnerability because many young people new to the scene feel pressured to use alcohol and other drugs or take them to reduce nervousness. This high use of drugs can increase health risks because the resulting loss of inhibition enables them to have sex and, often, unsafe sex. Some drugs such as amyl nitrate (poppers) can both heighten sexual pleasure and potentially increase the risk of practising unsafe sex.

'I think that certainly there's a lot of pressure on the scene – "be good in bed" type things – especially for young gay men where there's very much a stigma attached to it and often having a drink or using poppers or whatever helps you detach yourself from that. There's a lot of pressure out there to perform, and on the scene quite a lot of young people do sort of go out and get drunk, then they don't have to worry about it. I know the sort of people on the scene that use poppers and things like that to lower inhibitions and have an allegedly better time but they can't remember the next day.'
Young gay man, aged 17

Section Two
Education and support on sex, alcohol and other drugs

This section explores the education and support about sex, alcohol and other drugs that young people said they need. It also explores the opportunities and challenges that professionals identified in developing this work.

What young people told us

Throughout the project we asked young people and professionals about education and support on sex, alcohol and other drugs. The following offers an account of their experiences, wishes, anxieties and concerns in relation to education, health, support and care.

'We got first aid lessons at school, and got told how to safely jump out of a window if a building was on fire. It would have been so useful if they had thought about taking it further, to look at how to stay safe in general, maybe with something specific around alcohol and drugs. Teaching us things like the recovery position, how drugs or alcohol can affect your body. It's like now, whenever we go out it's like "Right, you need to drink this much water". If we didn't think someone was drinking enough water we'd say "Here's a bottle, drink some of that". It's also a case of drinking it slowly because you can also do yourself damage if you drink too much water. These are the things that save lives, not telling people about acts and legislations, because you need to know what to do if you or someone else is taken bad.'
Young man, aged 18

'Doing drugs is more like Year 10 or 11. Sex is Year 10, I think. Alcohol you start Year 8. You go out with all your friends and smoking in Year 7.'
Young woman, aged 18

'I remember we would have sex education about once a term, and then the police would come in and talk to us about drugs.'
Young woman, aged 18

Young people report getting 'a bit of sex education here, a bit of drug and alcohol education there' and that being all they can expect. This type of approach focuses on information provision and ignores coordinated skills development and exploration of values that underpin all emotional and social development work. They were clear that it is not just the responsibility of schools but that to be effectively supported they need opportunities to explore the issues at home, at school and in the community, with one-to-one support as well as health services.

We asked young people:

■ what they wanted to know and understand
■ what they want to be able to do
■ what they want to think about and explore.

They told us they need to know about:

■ how you know when you are ready for sex
■ whether and how alcohol and other drugs change the way you think about things and how they affect you
■ whether and how drugs can make you feel 'horny' and whether they can make sex better
■ what you can do if you are feeling pressured into having sex
■ whether and why you make bad decisions when you use alcohol and other drugs
■ how you can tell when you are drunk
■ whether alcohol and other drugs can make you have sex when you don't really want to
■ where they can go for help if they are worried
■ whether you will be judged if you go to a sexual health service for help and tell them you were drunk and so you made a mistake.

'It's like drugs and alcohol. If you don't give people the knowledge then they're going to want to go out and do it in order to get the knowledge and it just seems a really backward way of trying to teach people. If you give them the information then they can make the decisions.'
Young man, aged 17

They told us they need to be able to:

- talk to people about sex, alcohol and other drugs and access confidential help and support
- understand the different risks and be able to assess risks and manage them effectively
- plan in advance of a 'night out'
- recognise what they want and stick to their decisions even if they use alcohol and other drugs
- keep safe when they have used alcohol and other drugs.

They told us they want to think about and explore:

- real-life dilemmas such as who to tell if you are worried or ashamed about something you have done
- why decision-making is altered when you use alcohol and other drugs
- know and understand different people's beliefs about sex, alcohol and other drugs
- how to get help and support and manage your emotions if you have made a mistake, including mistakes made while drunk or using drugs
- why some people drink so much and have sex with 'anyone'
- different expectations of young men and young women.

'We need a chance to talk about our concerns about sex and drugs so that we can get all the inside information about the risks and what will happen.'
Young woman, aged 14

They also wanted to know how they can effectively inform and influence education and service provision so that it feels relevant and appropriate for them and addresses their needs.

They told us they wanted skilled and competent professionals.

'I went to the local clinic and I was really nervous because I needed emergency contraception because I forgot to use a condom. The nurse was really nice, she didn't judge me and she talked about how to try and make sure it didn't happen again.'
Young woman, aged 16

'I was lucky in that for a couple of years I had a teacher who was so sensitive and everyone loved her. You could just talk to her about anything at any time. She was so warm.'
Young man, aged 18

'When you went into the room it wasn't "Sit down, books out", it was "Hi everybody, how are you today?" and then she would talk to us on a one-to-one basis and also as a group. If anyone said anything then it wouldn't be like "Wait until the end and then ask questions". She would welcome the questions as they arrived and it just made you feel better about being in the room to start with.'
Young man, aged 20

Young people told us that professionals, including service staff, school nurses, teachers, learning mentors and social work staff, should:

- be good listeners
- be someone you can trust
- be down to earth
- make sessions interesting and fun
- not judge young people and their behaviour and should treat them like adults
- respect confidentiality and be clear when it is not available
- be relaxed and tell the truth including the negatives and the positives
- be understanding
- be interesting and humorous
- not preach
- be accessible, genuine, open, warm, friendly and patient
- not be patronising
- be comfortable talking about sex, relationships, drugs and alcohol
- be sensitive to diversity
- be there when you need them.

Young people's ideas for education settings

- spread the work out across the school timetable
- coordinate the lessons across year groups
- give us opportunities to explore issues – one-off lessons don't work
- have dedicated teachers and planned timetables
- we want visits from experienced external agencies too
- use distancing techniques such as case studies that allow for exploration without disclosure and feeling unsafe

- use videos to start discussing things we need to know
- use language we understand
- use young people and outside visitors
- work at a level we understand
- don't assume that we know everything about sex and drugs
- make it relevant to the reality of our lives.

what young
people say

'I remember we would have sex education about once a term and the police would come in and talk to us about drugs.'
Young man, aged 18

'I'd have a sex and drugs teacher in each school!'
Young woman, aged 17

'There should be a certain time each week in the timetable. Something that actually says "Not just here and there" – it should be set.'
Young man, aged 16

Young people's ideas for health, community and other settings

They also had a range of suggestions for professionals in different settings:

- make the work practical and hands on
- plan dedicated time/regular lessons
- provide leaflets and free stuff to take away (without having to ask!)
- make sure it is different from usual lessons
- involve and link work to services and agencies
- provide more discussion and in more detail
- start at a young age
- use language that is easy to understand
- offer opportunities to explore consequences
- make it thought provoking
- use interactive methods such as art, drama, role play and quizzes
- support us as peer educators
- be genuine
- ensure all the work is relevant to reality.

what young people say

'Because maybe if we could get told about it more and there is more detail, people would think more before they do things. We weren't told lots of detail, just "don't do that and don't do this". We weren't told why and what can happen.'
Young woman, aged 16

'I think the more adults tell children not to do things, the more they get curious to do it.'
Young woman, aged 16

'I think if someone is genuine with you and if someone is honest with you and tells you the good and tells you the bad then you're more likely to take in the good stuff, which is what I would have thought was the object of the situation. If you just drum into people "This is bad, this is bad, this is bad", which is unrealistic, they know that hundreds of thousands of people go out every night, have a few drinks, have a good time, go home completely safe.'
Young woman, aged 20

What professionals told us

Professionals confirmed that there is a continued separation between education and support regarding sex and relationships and alcohol and other drugs, although progress in service provision through one-stop shops was acknowledged. While most were committed to working with young people in a holistic way on sex, alcohol and other drugs, they identified a number of real or perceived barriers.

Being seen to condone sex, alcohol and other drugs

Integrating work on sex, alcohol and other drugs in this way is often perceived to be difficult because it requires workers to move away from a biological approach. Current policies in schools and other settings on sex and drugs are generally developed separately from each other which adds to the nervousness and fails to support the links being made.

'We have got to help them with the processing of all the stuff that comes at them so it is about what's actually correct, but also looking at being really careful that our messages are realistic and acceptable. I know people say "No, no, no, we have got to say no to them", but we have got to be credible and helpful and that can be quite a dilemma for those in authority.'
Health promotion worker

The importance of effective planning and preparatory work to secure support and commitment was emphasised.

Lack of confidence and skills

Professionals across disciplines stated a lack of confidence in their knowledge and competence to address the issues. They feared personal questions about sex, alcohol and other drugs, which they would not know how to manage, and were anxious they would not be considered credible or realistic by young people.

Lack of resources

Even though many were committed to exploring the issues they identified a lack of activities, resources and leaflets to help them.

what practitioners say

'We must avoid doomsday messages ... the reality is that young people will experiment with both sex and drugs so we need to tell them how to be safe when going about it.'
Teacher

The requests and issues raised by young people and professionals set a clear agenda for action. The implications for policy and practice are outlined in Section Three.

CASE STUDY

Engaging with young people about sex and relationships, drug and alcohol education in further education

Tacade worked with three further education/six form colleges in London while developing 'Sex, Drugs and Alcohol' material for use with young people aged 14 to 19. The student population attending these colleges was multicultural with a high proportion of young people from Black, Caribbean, African, South Asian, Turkish, Kurdish and white English communities.

We found there was a wide variety of opportunities to engage with young people about sex and relationships and drug and alcohol education in the college settings. Prior to developing the 'Sex, Drugs and Alcohol' materials, Tacade consulted students through ongoing health drop-ins run by local young people's sexual health services and at World AIDS Day stalls and events. The 'Sex, Drugs and Alcohol' materials were piloted with a variety of young people on GNVQ courses, through tutorials and with young people with special education needs attending life skills courses.

Through the work with colleges we found that students were very interested in drugs, alcohol and sexual health. But overall students' levels of knowledge and understanding were poor. In particular students did not have a clear understanding of sexual health issues such as HIV transmission and safer sexual practices. The majority of students we worked with had not had opportunities to consider the implications of drug and alcohol use on sexual behaviour within formal or informal education settings.

Through the work with colleges it became apparent that many staff required training and support to effectively deliver SRE, drug and alcohol education to students. Tutors at one college attended training about health education and were helped to develop the knowledge, skills and confidence to deliver SRE, drug and alcohol education to students. While all the staff found the training useful, some staff felt they required ongoing support and training, while other staff felt that health education should be taught by specialist workers.

Section Three
Promoting dialogue – the implications for policy and practice

This section reflects on the implications of the evidence from Sections One and Two for policy and practice. It offers issues for further dialogue between policy makers and practitioners.

Cultural change

Cultural change is necessary to engage openly and honestly with young people about sex and relationships, to help them to value themselves and others, and to stop providing mixed messages about sex, alcohol and drug use. Cultural change means addressing the realities of young people's lives and valuing them as independent decision-makers who need to be prepared to manage their lives now and in the future. We need to accept they will make mistakes, and they need education to prepare them for the range of different situations they may encounter. In doing this they can learn from their mistakes, grow and develop.

Development work with parents, carers and local communities will also make a significant contribution to bringing about cultural change. National and local campaigns that target young people, such as the campaign run by the Teenage Pregnancy Unit, also support cultural change by ensuring that young people know they can access confidential help and support and by putting out a public message that it is ok to be open about these issues.

Reproduced with permission from the Teenage Pregnancy Unit, Department for Education and Skills.

Developing education, services and support

We need to develop both mainstream and targeted provision of education, services and support for young people, with those who are marginalised and vulnerable receiving targeted support. This should build on the excellent examples of practice that already exist in many areas. Working in partnership is an effective way of ensuring targeted provision. Looked After Children's Nurses, Connexions personal advisors, youth and community workers, learning mentors, youth offending team workers, those in secure units and school and community nurses from PCTs are all in an ideal position to support targeted work with young people who are identified as vulnerable to increased risk-taking with potentially negative public health outcomes.

Professionals need to look beyond the immediate behaviours and understand the reasons why young people take risks, and use this understanding to inform the development of effective education, services and support.

Young people's participation

We need to further develop young people's participation. This work demonstrated the importance of listening to young people to ensure that education and support is relevant to them and their needs. Young people provide a clear mandate for this work. Developing effective participation is a key aspect of cultural change. Involving young people in decision-making and working with them to meet their needs will lead and facilitate cultural change in which we value their realities and opinions. The National Healthy School Standard document *Supporting Pupil Participation* (NHSS 2004 forthcoming) clarifies the breadth and scope of participation as well as practical strategies for its development. Across all settings there is now an expectation that children and young people will participate in decisions and the development of services.

what practitioners say

'A lot of time and energy could have been saved if we had looked at the issues together. The same issues apply about taking someone in our care to a sexual health service, as to a drug service. In the future I will look at bringing these issues together with other polices such as the HIV policy.'
Manager, Social Services

'We need a very clear framework of how we are going to do the work around the issues… I haven't seen anything that explicitly links the two.'
Teacher

Policy development

There is a need for holistic policies in all settings with clear and explicit values so workers have a framework and mandate for developing the links. This work challenges the current orthodoxy of maintaining separate policies for work on sex and relationships and alcohol and other drugs. We believe it is important that all policies relating to the promotion of the health and well-being of young people or PSHE and Citizenship are initially brought together in one folder with a covering statement that clarifies the links between different issues. As policies are reviewed over time, an overall policy can be developed which addresses all of the issues and includes appendices that clarify any particular issues or legal requirements. It is essential that policies identify the needs of all young people and address issues such as gender, faith and culture, disability, sexual orientation, ethnicity, literacy levels and how specific needs will be addressed within education and pastoral support. It should also reflect the organisation's Equal opportunities policy and also anti-bullying policies. It is essential when developing policy that it is agreed and endorsed by senior management as well as young people, parents, carers and others involved in the agency, school or institution and an action plan is developed to support its implementation. For schools, the local healthy schools programme will appropriately support development of this whole school approach. More information is available on www.wiredforhealth.gov.uk.

CASE STUDY

Drugs, Alcohol and Sexual Health Forum, Sheffield

Sheffield has a Drugs, Alcohol and Sexual Health Forum (DASH). This meets regularly to share information, consider areas of crossover in work and identify further possibilities for joint working. The Forum ran a conference in Spring 2003 which played a crucial role in highlighting the links between drugs, sex and alcohol across the city, and promoted the need for more collaboration between agencies.

The partnership has developed a substance misuse support service and a condom distribution scheme. They are now working on improving communication and distribution of information between drug and sexual health services as well as developing shared training and education. For example, building on the success of their national 'Sex, Drugs and Alcohol' course, the Forum is running this at a local level as well as developing training which specifically focuses on sexual health issues for drug and alcohol workers.

For more information contact the Centre for HIV and Sexual Health on 0114 226 1900 or visit www.sexualhealthsheffield.co.uk

Effective partnerships

Effective partnerships are key to successful outcomes for children. The Children, Young People and Families Directorate in the Department for Education and Skills aims to address the needs of children, young people and their families holistically. Partnerships across education, health, social care and the voluntary sector can ensure the sharing of local information, pooling of resources and the understanding of common objectives. It can also support skill development and the sharing of professional expertise and best practice. The development of joint objectives may contribute to school improvement aims and public health priorities such as drugs, alcohol, teenage pregnancy and sexual health. For example the drug action team coordinator may be concerned about binge drinking among young people, the teenage pregnancy coordinator may be concerned about the impact of binge drinking on sexual choices and behaviour and the youth offending team may be concerned about the impact of alcohol and other drugs on violence, aggression and criminal behaviour. Working together enables effective education, prevention and service provision.

Joined-up practice

We need to further develop 'joined up' Personal, Social Health Education and Citizenship, promotion of health and well-being and one-to-one support with an increased emphasis on linking the different issues in all contexts in which young people develop and grow. Young people tell us that at present education and support is often delivered as separate topics. Throughout this project young people and professionals emphasised the importance of developing personal and social skills that young people can use to ensure their personal safety, manage risks and improve their health and well-being.

The PSHE and Citizenship Frameworks in the National Curriculum Handbooks (QCA 1999a and 1999b) provide a planning tool for developing 'joined-up' work across all settings.

The Continuing Professional Development PSHE Certification programme is currently reviewing the separate modules on SRE and drug education to develop a more holistic certification programme. For further information contact Roz Caught at the NHSS Team (see Section Six).

Developing skills

A greater emphasis on developing young people's skills of risk-assessment and risk-management is needed to enable them to think about, understand and manage the risks they may take in relation to sex, alcohol and other drugs.

Local contexts

We must recognise the importance of local contexts including trends in behaviour. Throughout this project we came to understand that, even though there are some common factors among young people in different locations in relation to sex, alcohol and other drugs, there are

CASE STUDY

Using local knowledge

Through one-to-one interactions and comments 'around the club' a youth worker identified that many of the young people attending the club were drinking large amounts of alcohol and then having sex with members of their peer group.

Through their local sexual health-planning group she offered this information (keeping the identities of the young people anonymous) to health workers so they could use it to inform their consultations in sexual health services. As a result family planning staff asked questions as part of their consultations that enabled them to talk with young people about planning and preparation, sensible drinking and decision-making. The youth worker also worked to integrate exploration of the links within their ongoing sex and relationships education work.

also a number of differences. For example, why, how and where young people in rural areas take risks may be very different from why, how and where young people in urban areas take risks. Gathering local intelligence through service provision, health surveys and participation work with young people enables this understanding to be used to inform local education and services and clarify relevant and appropriate approaches.

Help and support

Young people must feel confident in getting help and support. Schools, youth services and residential care should promote service use and advertise services through:

- role play and case study work to explore the issues
- displaying posters and providing leaflets and helpline numbers
- including visits to and visits from services
- enabling quick referrals and, where necessary, transport to services
- explaining how helplines, websites and services work and what they can expect when they make contact

- on-site provision through a condom scheme, school nurse provision, weekly visit from health professionals
- peer education publicising services and the importance of using these.

Young people must be assured that they will be supported and helped without judgement by relevant professionals if they take sexual risks while using alcohol and other drugs.

Outside visitors can provide an effective link between formal and informal education and service provision. Where visitors are invited to assist they must work within the policy framework of the institution and it is the responsibility of those inviting the visitor to ensure this happens. Some organisations that provide outside visitors work from a moral and values framework that is not conducive to effective learning. Rather its aim is to shock and frighten children and young people. This is particularly true, for example, in relation to abortion. Some of these organisations provide factually incorrect information. This is clearly not acceptable as all the evidence from national and international research suggests we must have a positive view of sex and sexuality (Health Development Agency 2003), and work with young people on drugs is best done within the context of life skills.

Professional development

All people who work with young people require high-quality professional development opportunities where they can:

- clarify their own personal values and beliefs
- develop practical skills for supporting young people as they explore the links between sex, alcohol and other drugs
- develop practical skills for providing services and support that meets young people's needs.

Working with parents and carers

Many project are being developed to help parents and carers talk to their children about sex and relationships or drugs and alcohol. These include programmes and initiatives like Sure Start Plus, the fpa SpeakEasy project, Parentline Plus and Sheffield Parent to Parent Project. Work with parents and carers should support them in understanding and exploring the links between sex, alcohol and other drugs.

Section Four
Practical ideas for developing work on sex, alcohol and other drugs

This section offers practical suggestions for addressing the links between sex, alcohol and other drugs with young people. It provides a series of case studies and practical ideas. This section will be useful for practitioners wanting to develop the work across different settings.

Young people clearly identified what they need to know, understand and be able to do, if they are to manage the relationship between sex, alcohol and other drugs successfully. All work on emotional and social development should include three main elements:

■ acquisition of accessible, relevant and age-appropriate information
■ clarification and development of attitudes and values that support self-esteem and are positive to health and well-being
■ development of personal and social skills to enable emotional development and interaction with others as well as making positive health choices and actively participating in society.
(NCB 2003)

The following section offers a range of tried and tested ideas, strategies and activities for working with young people on sex, alcohol and other drugs in different settings. The activities/ideas can be used with young people aged 12 and over depending on their age, maturity and understanding.

One-to-one and outreach work

There are a range of people who work with young people in a one-to-one context and may offer general information and provide specific advice, support and help. These include Connexions personal advisors, learning mentors, health service staff, youth offending team workers, leaving care teams, school and community nurses, youth workers (including detached youth and outreach workers in pub and club work) and social workers. When providing support they can help young people think about how they can plan for and manage situations and potential risks effectively. We believe it would be useful to integrate questions about sex, alcohol and other drugs in any individual consultations and health assessments.

The Connexions service aims to provide integrated information, advice, guidance and personal development opportunities for all 13- to 19-year-olds in England. It also aims to help young people engage in learning, achieve their full potential and make a smooth transition to adult life. Connexions partnerships are actively involved in local teenage pregnancy and drug strategies. Connexions personal advisors work in a variety of settings with young people, both in and out of school. These include young people who may be homeless, teenage parents, those involved in or at risk of becoming involved in the criminal justice system, or those leaving care.

Those working in one to one confidential situations can disseminate their knowledge and understanding anonymously to inform the planning and delivery of more formal education within school or youth work settings, whilst at the same time ensuring young people know about relevant websites and helplines and have access to leaflets to take away with them.

CASE STUDY

The SWEET Project

SWEET is a club night event for minority ethnic young people under the age of 18 and their friends. Formed and delivered as a partnership between Sheffield Black Drugs Service and the Centre for HIV and Sexual Health the aim of the event is to raise awareness of drug, alcohol and sexual health services in Sheffield and to encourage black and minority ethnic young people to use them.

We know that young people may take risks with their sexual health when they are under the influence of drugs, including alcohol, and that many go on to regret such experiences. Alongside this are the complexities and cultural needs of BME communities, which sometimes means that drugs and sexual health are missed from the educational agenda.

SWEET provides a safe space for young people within a drug and alcohol free 'adult' environment where they can mix and build relationships with specially trained SWEET workers from the Black Drugs Service and the Centre for HIV and Sexual Health. Comprehensive sets of protocols and procedures have been drawn up to support all workers and young people involved in the project. SWEET workers are able, informally, to offer support, advice and information to young people and where necessary to follow up after the event on any issues raised during the evening.

SWEET takes place bi-monthly at a bar in the city centre. Young people can meet friends, get to know workers, listen to DJs or perform themselves, within a drug-free environment, demonstrating that relaxation and enjoyment are possible without alcohol on sale.

A video playing onto a large screen shows positive images of black young people from the media and this multimedia resource is also used to deliver information about drugs, alcohol and sexual health. A video box is available throughout the evening where young people can voice their opinions about the event or any of the issues which are being raised and promoted.

continued...

CASE STUDY

...continued

To sustain some of the learning and developments from the SWEET event, the team is able to follow up outside of the club event with group work for young people and training and support for workers. This also provides an opportunity to further promote the event and gather feedback and experiences of young people themselves.

For further information about SWEET or to find out about *The Directors* CD-ROM which provides detailed information about all aspects of the project, contact Lee Wisdom at Sheffield Black Drugs Service on 0114 249 3700 or Anne Shutt at the Centre for HIV and Sexual Health on 0114 226 1906.

CASE STUDY

The Safe in Sound Project

The Safe in Sound Project was set up in Southampton in 1997 as a response to recreational drug use in clubs and at music events. It was felt at the time that there was little relevant or accurate information being provided to the clubbing community about the impact that drug use could have on their lives in a legal or social context, and particularly on their health, including sexual health. Safe in Sound recognises that some people will use substances (including alcohol) as part of their night out and provides them with information that may help to reduce the potential risks.

The project is designed to be 'user-friendly' and approachable. Many of the volunteers who staff the project are involved in the club scene, so have valuable personal experience on top of the training provided by the project.

To meet its aims of raising awareness of the risks associated with substance use and reducing harm, the project carries out a number of activities. The main emphasis is on outreach work.

continued...

CASE
STUDY
...continued

This involves visiting a club, festival or music event and setting up an information point, usually at a quieter part of the event. The service is advertised through backdrops of the project logo and a series of posters with the wording 'free drugs information' ('information' being written considerably smaller than 'free drugs'). This, understandably, attracts a lot of attention from clients.

Around the information point we display various leaflets and booklets containing harm reduction information about a wide range of substances which clients can take away. Project volunteers wait for people to approach the information point before engaging in dialogue about any issues the client may wish to discuss. It is important to respect that people are primarily at the venue for a night out!

Substance use can cause young people to lose their inhibitions. This can sometimes lead to risky sexual behaviour. The project is therefore in an ideal position to promote sexual health through the provision of free condoms, lubricant and information about local sexual health services. Although Safe in Sound is not a counselling service, it can help people who may have deeper worries or concerns about their own, or a friend's, substance use or sexual health by referring them to a number of local agencies that can provide ongoing support, counselling or treatment.

For more information contact Rob Kurn on 023 8077 3461 or email r.kurn@southamptonvs.org.uk

Group work

It is commonly understood that active learning methods are the most effective approach to working with groups on emotional and social issues. This section explores some ideas for working in groups on sex, alcohol and other drugs. For general information about using active learning methods and creating a safe learning environment see Sex Education Forum Factsheet 12 Effective Learning, available free on www.ncb.org.uk/sef.

All work on sex, alcohol and other drugs needs to include the three main elements of:

1. knowledge and understanding
2. personal and social skills
3. values and beliefs including emotions.

The following offers ideas about how these elements can be addressed and some practical examples.

Knowledge and understanding

Knowledge and understanding can be developed through quizzes, questionnaires and research (including using the Internet). The Sex, alcohol and other drugs quiz on page 43 was developed by Max Biddulph and has been used successfully to stimulate discussion about the links between sex, alcohol and other drugs with young people. It should not be used as a test of knowledge, rather as a stimulus for discussion. This quiz can be photocopied and used with groups of young people.

Sex, alcohol and other drugs quiz

No.	Question	True	False	It depends
1	The UK now has more 15- and 16-year-old drug users than any other country in the European Union (EU).			
2	The UK's teenage pregnancy rate is starting to fall.			
3	One in seven 16–24 year olds reports having had unprotected sex after having drunk alcohol; one in 10 is unable to remember if they had sex the night before.			
4	Alcohol and other drugs can make people around you seem more sexy, interesting and appealing.			
5	Sex will always be more pleasurable if you use alcohol and other drugs.			
6	If you are dancing in a club and have taken ecstasy it is important to drink water.			
7	Some young people use alcohol and other drugs because they are dealing with distressing emotional issues such as bullying, low self-esteem and feeling bad about their body.			
8	Young gay men and women are more likely to use alcohol and other drugs than any other group of young people.			
9	Some people deliberately 'spike' the drinks of others so that they can take advantage of them sexually.			
10	Remembering to take condoms with you when you go out at the start of the night will help to protect you from possible unsafe sex later.			
11	Some people drink alcohol in social situations, e.g. a club because they do not have the confidence to chat people up or socialise when they are sober.			
12	The next day when they realise that they have had unsafe sex most young people are not bothered.			

Sex, alcohol and other drugs quiz: answers and discussion points for practitioners

No.	Answer
1	True. Discussion Point: Why do they think this is?
2	The UK's teenage pregnancy rate is starting to fall but it remains the highest in Western Europe. Discussion Point: What do they think can be done to reduce it still further?
3	Research shows that young people often have unprotected sex after they have drunk alcohol or used other drugs. Discussion Point: Why do people have unprotected sex when they use alcohol and other drugs?
4	Alcohol and other drugs can make people around you seem sexier and more interesting. Discussion Point: Why do you think this happens? What is the possible impact of this?
5	Some people believe that alcohol and other drugs improve sexual pleasure. Many people do not like being 'smashed' and having sex. Discussion Point: Why might some people like being 'smashed'?
6	It is important to drink enough water when taking ecstasy and dancing. However too much water can be dangerous too. There are leaflets which young people can access that offer recommended amounts of water to drink. Contact DrugScope for more information. www.drugscope.org.uk
7	Evidence from research and practice tells us that they sometimes use sex, alcohol and other drugs to help them feel better about themselves. Discussion Point: Why might alcohol and other drugs seem to help? Will they help in the long term?
8	Some research and evidence from practice suggests that this is true. The commercial gay scene often focuses on sex, alcohol and other drugs and many young men and women who are gay use drugs to improve their confidence and fit in. Discussion Point: Why do you think this is true? Is it the same for other marginalised groups?
9	There is some research and evidence from practice that suggests this does happen and increasingly it is becoming a focus for concern with some areas running campaigns to raise awareness. Discussion Point: Why do you think some people do this?
10	Being prepared is an important step and if someone thinks they are going to have sex it is important to take condoms and plan to use them. Discussion Point: How can people be prepared?
11	Evidence from research and practice shows that using alcohol and other drugs can improve people's confidence and help them in social and sexual situations. Discussion Point: What strategies are there for improving confidence?
12	Most young people do care; however they may not have the confidence or trust to access services for a range of reasons including being judged by professionals for making a mistake. Discussion Point: How can people try and avoid this situation? How can they find out about services if they need them?

CASE STUDY

Exploring the links in a Pupil Referral Unit

One mixed gender group of young people, aged 15 and 16, who were permanently excluded from school and attending a Pupil Referral Unit identified the impact of alcohol and drugs on sexual behaviour as an area they wanted to explore. Through involving them, interest was secured and two young people agreed to develop a quiz and research the answers. The following week they ran the session, using the quiz as a stimulus for a whole-group discussion. They concluded that, even though some of them enjoyed alcohol and drugs, they needed to be careful about the impact of their use on their ability and desire to practise safer sex. One of the young people submitted the quiz as part of their portfolio of work for English Language.

Developing personal and social skills

The development of personal and social skills includes the ability to make, and act upon, accurate judgements about risk, decision-making, negotiation, managing influences and pressures. Developing skills is crucial as, even with the best information possible, young people cannot use this information if they do not have well-developed personal and social skills. Pactitioners can use their understanding from local and national research and participation work with young people to develop authentic and locally relevant scenarios that address skills and values.

Scenarios, role play and case studies are a useful method for developing skills in an impersonal and non-threatening way.

Using scenarios to explore issues

The ASDAN Sex and Relationships Education Resource works within a key skills context. It offers the following scenario to help develop decision-making and negotiation skills in relation to sex, alcohol and other drugs. This scenario provides a model for others to adapt and develop depending on the local context, and the maturity and understanding of the young people you are working with.

Jane and Max are going to the school disco together. Jane wants Max to drink some cider before they get there. Max does not want to and does not want Jane to either. In pairs, young people are asked to role-play the scenario as a way of thinking through the issues and developing practical negotiation skills.

Once the role-plays have been completed, questions such as the ones below can be asked to help young people process the learning.

How can they resolve any conflicts between what they think and feel to ensure they take the best course of action?

What might be the emotional and physical consequences of their different decisions?

Further details about the ASDAN resource are on page 73.

The following case study outlines how role play is used in a young offender institution to build young people's confidence and skills in accessing help and support.

CASE
STUDY

Linking the issues in a youth offender institution

During sex and relationships education at Aycliffe Young People's Centre we have a one-hour session and role play attending a GUM clinic. A young person has a night out with his friends and becomes intoxicated, has unprotected sex and catches a Sexually Transmitted Infection (STI). Another young person shares his friend's needle and syringe to inject drugs and becomes HIV positive.

A role-play scenario is developed where these young people attend an imaginary GUM clinic and explore what happens. Once the characters have deroled, a discussion takes place with the audience about the role of alcohol and its effects on sexual decision-making. This may include a wider discussion about respect, morals, love, trust, feelings, how different cultures view sex and alcohol, and access to services. Other activities include discussions on STIs and HIV, sharing needles, and developing 'feel, think and do' scenarios where young people have had unprotected sex under the influence of alcohol/drugs. Again, the emphasis is on exploring choices and accessing support. Ayecliffe Young People's Centre has an SRE Group and a Drug, Alcohol and Substance Misuse Group who work together to develop and deliver these sessions.

The Drug and Alcohol Group runs a session in conjunction with the SRE Group on 'HIV, AIDS and Drug Use'. The SRE Group also has a session about sex, pregnancy and responsibility, using scenario cards, one of which covers alcohol and drugs and sex.

For more information contact Joan Hughes at Ayecliffe Young People's Centre on 01325 300101.

The following case study clarifies the importance of moving beyond information, to providing opportunities for skills development.

CASE
STUDY

Saturday Night Out

Saturday Night Out was developed as an activity in schools in Croydon as part of PSHE and Citizenship. This was in response to an identified need to move away from the 'biological', to involve discussions of emotions/feelings and development of negotiating/decision-making skills.

Saturday Night Out enables the group to look at relationships, negotiating skills and contraceptive use by creating characters and scenarios that may feature during a night out. Young people are given a set of options and dilemmas and work out what the characters need to do to keep safe but still enjoy themselves.

It is now used with groups of young people, and also when training professionals who are working with young people, to raise awareness of:

- alcohol and drug use related to sexual health
- sexual health issues, particularly emergency contraception and condom use
- personal safety issues, decision-making and negotiating skills
- where to go for help/advice and support services locally.

For more information contact Karin O'Sullivan at Croydon Teenage Pregnancy on 020 8680 2008

The following activity is based on the *Satuday Night Out* work developed in Croydon. It aims to provide an opportunity to think about decision-making, assertiveness and peer influence.

Guided visualisation

This visualisation is based on the work developed by Karin O'Sullivan. It can be used as a guided visualisation for those who are confident in using this technique, or can be adapted and used as a case study. It explores how alcohol can affect sexual decision-making.

Method

1. Explain the purpose of the activity. (The following is a suggested introduction.)

   This is an activity designed to help you explore how alcohol impacts on sexual decision-making at a party. We will be going through a guided visualisation where I will describe events at a party. If any of you have experienced this type of event, it may remind you of it. Remember you are always in control of the situation. If you feel uncomfortable, remind yourself that you are in control. If you want to, you can always bring your attention back to the room at any point and simply stop the imagery. You will not be asked to share anything from your experience that you do not want to.

2. Take them through the guided visualisation. Read slowly, give participants time to visualise some of the thoughts and situations. Let about 10 seconds pass between paragraphs.

Visualisation

■ Start by closing your eyes to block out distractions and help focus your thoughts. I will be reading this guided imagery to you. It will take a few minutes. As I read, try to be aware of how you are thinking, how you are feeling, what are you thinking.

■ As you sit in your chair, make sure both your feet are flat on the floor. Place your hands in a comfortable position. Now, take a deep breath, hold it and then slowly release it … do that again… Continue at your own pace.

continued...

...continued

- Imagine you are on your way to a party with your friends. Notice what you are wearing and who you are with.

- On your way, your group decides to stop at the off licence and get some alcohol. Notice what you are feeling and what you are thinking. What do you decide to do? Think about what happens between the off licence and the party.

- You get to the party, the music is good and everyone is laughing and enjoying themselves. Notice whether you are enjoying yourself. Notice if you feel comfortable and confident. Notice what your friends are doing.

- One of your friends is really, really drunk. Someone they have always fancied is chatting them up. Notice how you feel and what you are thinking. What do you do?

- They come over to you and say that they are going outside together. Notice how you feel and what you are thinking. What do you do?

3. After a few moments ask people to open their eyes and bring their attention back to the room. Divide into groups of four or five and ask the young people to think about:

- What was it like to go through the process?
- What do you remember about how you felt at different stages?
- Were there any conflicts between the way you felt, what you thought and what you did?
- How did you make your choice at the off licence?
- Did using or not using alcohol affect any of the evening's 'events'? If so, how?
- Do you think your thoughts, feelings and choices might have been different if you were a member of the opposite sex?
- Did anything surprise you?
- What did you learn?
- Having done this exercise, will you change anything in the future?

As identified earlier, young people with learning difficulties may need additional help and support to enable them to understand the links between sex, alcohol and other drugs. The following case study demonstrates how the issues can be addressed with this group of young people.

CASE STUDY

Working on the links between alcohol and sex at Red Lodge School

Red Lodge is a school for young people aged 11 to 16 with mild to moderate learning difficulties.

PSHE and Citizenship is delivered using illustrations, cartoons, worksheets, case studies (think, feel and do responses) and exercises which are built on from year to year.

The young people attending the school are familiar with popular drinks such as 'alco-pops'. These are used in discussion about how they might make you feel different. Cartoon depictions of two drunk, smiley characters entering a bedroom are used to prompt discussion on what might happen next. Issues of safety and coercion are covered using 'OK' and 'Not OK' exercises. The whole class then work together and discuss their ideas and explore the most effective strategies.

The environment is bright, warm and safe. Working agreements are always developed at the beginning of lessons. Pictures and symbols such as word and thought bubbles are used to ask 'What should characters do in this situation?' The whole class then discusses this.

For more information contact Celia Bowden on 023 8078 7988.

Values and beliefs

In order to be truly meaningful and effective, work must explore the range of societal, cultural, group and individual values and beliefs that people hold about drug use and sexual behaviour.

As well as developing practical skills through role play it is important to help young people connect to potential emotional and cognitive responses, and help them develop the ability to use their thinking skills with their emotions to inform behaviour. Developing 'think, feel and do' scenarios gives young people opportunities to engage with values, beliefs, emotions and identify issues such as using alcohol and drugs to build confidence, body image, or taking drugs because others are.

Offering scenarios with associated questions, such as the following, provides an opportunity to explore emotions, values and beliefs.

Exploring emotions, values and beliefs

Present the following scenario to small groups of young people. Ask them to discuss the following questions.

Lindy is 15 and goes to a party one night with her friends. The night is going really well and she gets chatting to Eddie, whom she has just met. She wakes up in bed with him the next morning and can't remember what happened.
■ What might Lindy be feeling?
■ Why might she not be able to remember what happened?
■ What might Eddie be thinking?
■ What might her parents and friends be thinking?
■ What might be the consequences of their actions?
■ Where can they get help and advice?

Group work is likely to raise issues for individuals that cannot be addressed publicly and therefore providing other sources of support is important.

Values and beliefs 'runaround' exercise

Aim

To explore the range of beliefs and values about sex, alcohol and other drugs.

This can be done using signs placed at strategic points in a room with the words 'Agree', 'Slightly agree', 'Not sure', 'Slightly disagree' and 'Disagree' written on them – having five headings allows for a greater spectrum of discussion and means that the areas are less crowded physically. A series of statements is read out one at a time, such as:

- Having a couple of drinks can make you feel more sexy
- It's easier to talk to someone you fancy if you use alcohol and other drugs
- Drinking lots of alcohol can give you 'brewer's droop'
- Using alcohol and other drugs can make sex more enjoyable
- Ecstasy can make everyone look more gorgeous
- Drinking beer makes young men look more macho and exciting
- Having sex when you are drunk is a bad thing
- Young women who go out and get drunk are asking for it
- Some religions forbid the use of alcohol and other drugs

Alternatively young people can write down any ideas, views, beliefs and myths about the links between sex, alcohol and other drugs to help you develop statements. The aim is not to get right or wrong answers but rather to stimulate discussion and thought.

'Like, if you're having problems, or if you want to find out information or just want somebody to talk to about sex and stuff, say you might not understand some stuff, so you need some person that you can go to and ask questions.'
Young man, aged 15

The values and beliefs exercise provides an opportunity for young people to hear and think about the range of different beliefs and values others hold about sex, alcohol and other drugs. When facilitating exercises such as this it is important that misconceptions, prejudices and discrimination are challenged creatively.

Information can be provided for young people to take away to reinforce what has been covered during sessions. Some young people find it difficult to ask for specific information and would like it to be given out in leaflet form to everyone as part of a lesson.

It is also important for young people to know who they can speak to or ask questions of privately. Local and in-house services (e.g. one-stop shops, helplines, clinics, school counselling) need to be easy for young people to access. Some young people may need occasional or ongoing support and will talk to their Connexions personal advisor, social worker or relevant support in school.

Using arts and creative approaches

'I found that a good way of dealing with taboo issues was in drama class. We had a really good drama teacher who was so relaxed she insisted that we called her by her first name. So we knew her as a person. She was a bit wacky, a bit funky, and a bit funny!'
Young man, aged 16

Art and creative approaches connect fantasy and emotion with thinking skills and enable young people to explore issues and practise new skills confidently in a distanced way.

Theatre in education is one positive way of exploring issues, as demonstrated in the following Theatre in Education case study.

Theatre in Education

Stockport LEA gained funding to support the development of a Theatre in Education play focusing on the links between sex, alcohol and other drugs. The play is about a party where young people are drinking, using cannabis and other drugs (ecstasy is offered). The characters speak their thoughts out loud to the audience, expressing their uncertainty, lack of knowledge, skills and confidence to deal with the situations which they encounter, i.e. peer pressure, lowering of inhibitions, the risks and consequences of their decisions. The couple who have sex at the party explore their emotions and reactions. The play also explores attitudes and values among young people, including 'reputations' (slag, Jack the lad, etc.), while also emphasising the consequences of the young person's actions not just for themselves, but for friends and families, including the impact on the teenage mum's education, career and future relationship opportunities. (In the play, the young couple do not have a relationship after the party.) It also highlights the lack of education, both from school and home, that young people have on the issues of sex, relationships and drugs.

Following the play, the audience gets the chance to question the characters in role and follow-up work is done in the classroom, using the teaching pack and any other resources which the teacher feels appropriate.

A video of the play and supporting teacher's pack has been produced and is available from Stockport LEA.

A good practice guide for using Theatre in Education, *It Opened My Eyes*, is available from the Health Development Agency.

Creative approaches can be developed and used within one-to-one and group contexts and are particularly helpful for working with young people who are disengaged from learning or have low literacy levels.

Creative approaches to exploring issues

The following ideas have been used with young people in a range of settings.

- Develop a poster or leaflet campaign to help young people understand the links between sex, alcohol and other drugs.

- Develop, practise and perform a short role-play/drama sketch about two young people or a group of friends who go to a party and use alcohol and other drugs. Role-play a positive experience and a negative experience.

- Write an advert for a radio or television campaign about the reasons young people should think about the links between sex, alcohol and other drugs.

- Role-play a meeting of the Teenage Pregnancy Partnership Board or local council meeting where the aim is:
  - to identify the issues
  - to work out what education, prevention and support needs to be in place to help young people
  - to decide how to attract young people more successfully to local services.

- Collect a range of magazines, coloured paper, paints, etc., and ask the group to work in pairs or small groups to develop a collage which addresses the following questions:
  - Why do young people use alcohol and other drugs to help them have sex?
  - What might be the positive and negative consequences of this?

- Design a leaflet explaining to parents and carers why they need to talk to their children about the links between alcohol, drugs and sexual behaviour, including some advice about what, when and how they could address the issue.

The following case study demonstrates how drama and role play can be used to help vulnerable young people explore the links between sex, alcohol and other drugs.

CASE STUDY

The Flower 125 Health Club

The Flower 125 Health Club is a multi-agency project, which delivers health workshops to vulnerable young people aged 11 to 16 years. The programme of workshops covers a variety of topics including sexual health, alcohol, healthy eating and smoking.

The underlying philosophy of the work is to raise self-esteem through the use of a model of giving praise and rewards. In 2000 the programme was extended and young people who had previously participated in the work received training as peer educators and now help to deliver the programme.

The programme takes place over 10 weeks, with an optional residential weekend. Some of the exercises include:

- Discussion of how alcohol and drugs can affect the body, judgement and decision-making.
- Sexual health, drug and alcohol quizzes.
- Whose responsibility is it anyway? Scenarios looking at decision-making, responsibilities, choices and consequences.

Young people have an opportunity to explore the issues regarding sex, alcohol and other drugs through the use of drama, looking at the potential benefits and consequences of combining them. Techniques include Forum Theatre (where young people stop the drama and discuss what might happen next), hot seating (where actors are asked questions in role by the audience), sculpting (where young people act out an emotion felt in a particular situation), and creating characters. Forum Theatre is interactive and can be offered as a group exercise or alongside a performance with an audience.

For more information contact Siobhan McFeely on 0114 226 4744 or email siobhan.mcfeely@sheffieldn-pct.nhs.uk

Developing skills of participation, enquiry and research

These ideas can be used in one-to-one and group settings in school and the community with young people aged 12 plus. The focus is on young people's active participation in their own learning. In the context of schools these support the aims of Citizenship.

The formal Citizenship curriculum within schools requires that children and young people study, reflect upon and discuss topical, moral, social and cultural issues. It requires that they can express their own views and listen to the views of others. It also requires that pupils develop as active citizens and participate in decisions that affect them. In informal settings it can also provide opportunities for young people to explore the issues.

Role play

1. Explain that there is a local teenage pregnancy strategy and a local drug strategy. The Drug Action Team (DAT) coordinator and the Teenage Pregnancy (TP) coordinator have arranged a meeting with the school/PRU/Connexions advisor to discuss the relationships between sex, alcohol and other drugs.

2. Ask one person to role play the TP coordinator, one to role-play the DAT coordinator, and one to role-play the teacher, etc. The rest of the group watch a meeting where they are asked to decide the role of schools, parents and youth service, and the media in developing awareness of the issues among young people.

3. Observers can stop the 'meeting' and offer advice and support or ideas or swap seats with one of the group.

4. Complete the exercise by writing a note to teachers, parents, carers, TP and DAT coordinators offering them six points on how they should work with young people on sex, alcohol and other drugs.

The Teenage Pregnancy and Drug Action Team coordinators could be invited in to run this meeting 'for real'.

Young people can undertake research projects and present their findings to the class, set up display boards, or present to assemblies, including community assemblies, youth groups and local councillors. They can also present to a governors' meeting as part of curriculum review, or to the Primary Care Trust or Local Partnership Board.

These activities help young people develop skills and values to participate effectively in their learning, and provide positive opportunities for them to develop their own understanding of the range of issues relating to drugs and sexual behaviour. They also provide opportunities for adults to understand the realities of some young people's lives.

Ideas for research and development projects

Young people can be asked to research a wide range of topics such as the ones below.

- Develop a young person's guide to government policy on sex, alcohol and other drugs and its relevance to young people.

- Community and identity – What are the local issues for young people in relation to sex, alcohol and other drugs? Do many young people binge drink? Does this impact on their sexual behaviour? What support is available for young people in my area?

- What are the causes of teenage pregnancy? What role do alcohol and other drugs play in teenage pregnancy and sexual ill health?

- Gender and decision-making – Are there different issues for young men and women when it comes to sex, alcohol and other drugs? Why is this?

- Disability, sex, alcohol and other drugs – What information is given to young people with disabilities about sex and relationships and the impacts of alcohol and drugs? Are they given sufficient information? If not, why?

continued...

...continued

- Culture, ethnicity and behaviour – How does culture, ethnicity and faith impact on people's behaviour in relation to sex, alcohol and other drugs?

- Gay and lesbian young people – Evidence shows that some gay and lesbian young people are more likely to use alcohol and other drugs, particularly on the 'gay scene'. Why do you think this is? What might be the impact on their sexual behaviour?

- Getting help and advice – What support services exist in my area? What is good and bad about them? Can I get to them easily? What times are they open? Are the staff friendly? Are the services confidential? Do they address the link between sex, alcohol and other drugs?

Peer work and active citizenship

Peer work and active citizenship means working with young people as partners and utilising their knowledge, skills, experience and peer influence in a positive, planned and structured way. It can help support, inform and develop the skills, understanding, confidence and self-awareness of other children and young people with whom they work with.

Peer work is increasingly popular in all settings where young people develop and grow. It can include peer mentoring, listening, buddying and education. There are examples in England and internationally of young people being trained and supported as peer educators and working on projects that address sex, alcohol and other drugs.

The following case study from New Zealand offers an example of peer led work on sex alcohol and other drugs.

Alcohol and other Drugs Workshop – Peer Sexuality Support (PSS) Project, Auckland, New Zealand

As part of their training, 30 Peer Sexuality Support students are taken on a five-day live-in training camp in the bush. During this time, workshops are facilitated on a number of topics relating to sexual health, including alcohol and other drugs, and their relationship to sexual decision-making.

These alcohol and other drugs workshops are run from a harm-minimisation perspective, and the difference between 'use' and 'abuse' is clarified. For example, having a glass of wine with dinner once a fortnight is use, having a litre of wine with breakfast is abuse. A range of information is provided about the effects of various drugs, including alcohol. The students include their own knowledge about the effects of different drugs, and what happens to their body, mind and emotions.

Students also talk about what they think the benefits of alcohol and other drugs are, for example, 'It makes me feel brave about approaching someone at a party'; 'It makes me feel like I fit in'; 'It makes me feel I can tell good jokes'.

Discussion then begins about some of the possible impacts of alcohol and other drugs on sexual decision-making, like having sex with someone you didn't want to, having sex with someone you like but not using condoms, being vulnerable to non-consensual sex. The students contribute their ideas, including things they have heard that may have happened to people who were using and abusing alcohol and other drugs.

Using brainstorming, a number of scenarios are then developed from this information where young people take alcohol and drugs, for example, at a party, at a friend's place, at school or at a club. The students are divided into groups of six, and devise a role-play. Each group works on an effect of alcohol and other drugs on sexual decision-making in a particular scene, and performs it for the rest of the group. Each role-play lasts about 10 minutes.

continued...

CASE STUDY

...continued

After the role-plays, the whole group discusses the situation in each role-play, and what could have been done differently. A whole range of ideas are gathered, including, 'Getting a sober friend to keep an eye on you'; 'Making sure you have enough money to get a taxi home so you don't need to ask for a ride'; 'Keeping your taxi money in a separate place from your other money, so it doesn't get spent'; 'Having the phone number of a taxi company, or of someone who has earlier agreed to pick you up, written down'; 'Staying with people you trust and not going off by yourself with someone'.

This workshop is done in conjunction with others, such as negotiating skills, values and beliefs (self-respect), safer sex, etc. Students appreciate the non-judgemental attitude of facilitators, and being taught skills that enable them to live in and work with their communities and environments, rather than against them.

Kim Elliot, Peer Sexuality Support Coordinator

For further information visit www.everybody.co.nz/sexfiles/pss.htm

Young people as evaluators of services

A number of areas have developed mystery shopper projects, where young people are trained to visit services anonymously and then provide feedback to the services about areas that are good and areas for development. Young people can be trained to ask questions related to the use of alcohol and other drugs in sexual relationships to ascertain whether services provide positive treatment of young people in relation to these issues. Young people then provide feedback to services to help the services improve their approach. Further information about mystery shopping approaches is available from the Centre for HIV and Sexual Health (see Useful organisations, page 75), who have produced the video *Undercover uncovered*.

Using new technologies

Information and Communication Technology (ICT) is increasingly becoming an important and effective medium for developing work around sex, alcohol and other drugs. The Web can be used as a way of researching ideas and information about the issues for a research/development task. For example, young people use the Internet to identify the impact of alcohol and drugs on decision-making or find out how they affect sexual arousal. Some relevant sites include:

www.ruthinking.org.uk
www.trashed.co.uk
www.frank.co.uk

There is a range of CD-ROMs that address sex, alcohol, and other drugs including *Sense, Sex and Relationships for 14–16 year olds* and *The Scene*, outlined in the following two case studies.

CASE
STUDY

Sense, Sex and Relationships for 14–16 year olds

Sense, Sex and Relationships for 14–16 year olds explicitly addresses the relationship between sex, alcohol and other drugs by following animated characters at a party.

There is a supporting manual with ideas for follow-up activities in the classroom or less formal settings. After they have looked at the CD-ROM, young people are asked to consider the following questions:

■ Why do some people drink alcohol or take drugs when they are thinking about having sex?
■ What are the possible benefits for them?
■ What are the possible negative consequences?
■ When people drink alcohol or take drugs and are thinking about having sex what do they need to think about beforehand?
■ Where can they get help and advice?

For further information see Section Six or visit www.sense.cds for a preview

The Scene

The Scene is a video/CD-ROM made by young people who are lesbian, gay, bisexual and transgender (LGBT) for use in secondary schools, youth centres and other settings.

The Scene lasts for 25 minutes and describes the journey of nine young people around the gay commercial pub and club scene. Initially it all appears to be bright, exciting and fun for the young people involved. Everyone is out drinking, flirting and enjoying themselves. However, the focus changes and the film goes on to interview each of the young people about the issues they have faced both prior to and since coming on to the scene and helps break down myths and stereotypes about young LGBT people.

Young people talk about 'coming out' (telling others that they are lesbian, gay or bisexual), about the mix of excitement and nervousness when going out on to the scene for the first time, and about the importance of friendships and adopting safety strategies.

The film features one young man describing how he did not receive effective sex education at school. In his attempts to discover himself, he became involved in alcohol and drugs with older men, who sexually exploited him. Others talk about being 'out' at work, about being transgender and about the pressures they feel when out in an environment where sex, alcohol and drugs are commonplace.

The film was made at the suggestion of the young people attending the BreakOut Youth Project in Southampton. They felt it was important to educate other young people (both gay and straight) on what coming out means, and on the risks and realities of being out in an adult environment.

The young people identified the need, developed the script and were involved in the editing of the film, which was premiered in the presence of the Mayor of Southampton at BreakOut's tenth birthday party.

This resource can be used as a trigger for discussion on a range of issues including sex, alcohol and drug use on the commercial gay scene.

For more information contact BreakOut Youth Project on 023 8022 3344 or visit www.breakoutyouth.co.uk

Section Five
Continuing professional development

This sections addresses continuing professional development and outlines a half-day professional development session.

Work is best delivered by people who feel confident and skilled. All workers have an entitlement to ongoing professional development. There is a variety of ways to develop confidence and skills, ranging from private reflection to formal certification.

Private reflection

Effective practitioners are those who reflect on their knowledge, skills and understanding. The following questions have proved helpful in preparation and evaluation.

■ What do I already know that will support me in working on sex, alcohol and other drugs? What more do I need to know? How will I acquire that knowledge?
■ What skills do I have that will enable effective facilitation of these issues? How can I get support to develop any potential gaps?
■ What beliefs and values do I hold that will support or work against effective delivery of this work?
■ What is the values framework of my institution and how should I incorporate it in my work with young people on sex, alcohol and other drugs?

'We need a very clear framework of how we are going to do the work around the issues.'
PSHE teacher

Evaluation of work

- What did I do well?
- What did I not do so well?
- What would I do differently next time?
- Did we meet the learning outcomes set for the group?
- How did the group feel about the exercise?
- How can I use this learning to support future planning?
- Is there any learning for colleagues? If yes, how will I share it?

Some practitioners have found it helpful to work in pairs or threes to reflect upon work and offer support and challenge.

Team work

Working in partnership with another colleague enables the development of skills and confidence. It is particularly helpful if:

- both workers are working in new areas (as this work will be for many practitioners)
- one worker has limited confidence or is less experienced than another
- workers have different expertise and skills that complement each other.

Working together enables the sharing of skills, support and clarification and is best utilised when time is spent planning and carefully debriefing to capture the learning.

Staff team training

Whole teams developing their expertise together is an effective way of ensuring consistency and an agreed framework for education and support. The activity on page 68 can be used individually, in staff meetings or together in a half-day or one-day session.

Formal training

Training and support may be available through local healthy schools programmes, the local education authority, the Primary Care Trust and voluntary organisations.

The National Children's Bureau runs a one-day course 'Sex, drugs and alcohol – exploring the links'. For more information contact training@ncb.org.uk

TACADE, fpa and the Centre for HIV and Sexual Health also offer training on the links between sex, alcohol and other drugs. (See Section Six).

PSHE certification

The DfES and Department of Health, through the National Healthy School Standard, have developed a PSHE certification process for teachers and community nurses. This explicitly acknowledges the need to develop an understanding of and competence in exploring the links between drugs, choices and sexual behaviour.

For further information contact the National Healthy School Standard (see Section Six).

A half-day session

This short programme has been used with a range of professionals including those working with young offenders, with young people who are being sexually exploited, with young carers and in education settings.

Time: Three hours

Outcome:

By the end of the session participants will:
■ understand the importance of, and evidence base for, working with young people on the links between sex, alcohol and other drugs
■ have identified and explored personal and professional opportunities and challenges for developing the work
■ have developed an action plan for developing practice in their setting.

Outline:

1. Opening round – who we are, where from?

2. Working agreement – ask the group to decide a working agreement for the rest of the day. It could include statements such as:
   ■ listen to each other
   ■ disagree/challenge respectfully
   ■ be punctual.

3. Short presentation on the research and evidence base for linking work on sex, alcohol and other drugs (use the information in Section One). Allow time for questions and a group discussion.

4. Break

5. Ask participants to work in pairs or groups of three to identify personal and professional opportunities and challenges in developing work that explores the links between sex, alcohol and other drugs.

   Ask the participants to write these on the reflection matrix (page 70). The questions on the prompt sheet (page 71) will help them identify their opportunities and challenges.

   Allow about 45 minutes for participants to complete this task.

6. In the whole group, ask participants to share some key points from their matrix. Identify and discuss key recurring themes.

7. Ask participants to work in pairs to discuss how they can make the most of their opportunities and how they can address the challenges they identified.

   Ask participants to develop an action plan for taking forward work that links sex alcohol and drugs. Participants should think about:
   ■ what they need to do in the short term and the medium term
   ■ participation, partnerships, policy and practice.

8. Closing round: ask participants to share one thing that they will take away from the day.

Reflection matrix

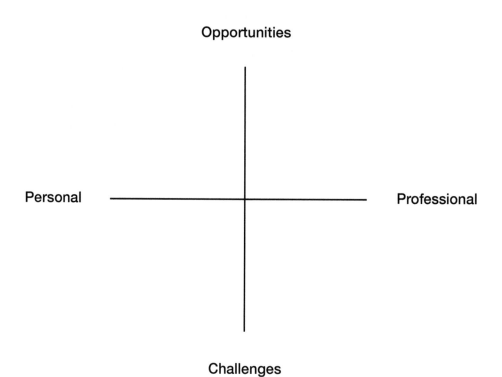

Opportunities

Personal ———————————— Professional

Challenges

Prompt questions for reflection matrix

■ What personal beliefs and values do I hold that support this work?

■ What professional beliefs and values do my organisation and I have that support this work?

■ What skills and qualities do I and others in my organisation have that support this work?

■ What personal beliefs and values do I hold that may challenge me in this work?

■ What professional beliefs and values do my organisation or I have that may challenge me in this work?

■ What skills do I and/or others in my organisation need to develop to deliver this work effectively?

■ What opportunities do I have now and what opportunities can I create?

Section Six
Useful resources and organisations

Resources and further reading

Sinclair, N (2002) *Alcohol and Teenage Pregnancy: Briefing paper*.
Alcohol Concern

The briefing paper has been written for all those involved in personal, social and health education with young people in schools or youth work settings, such as PSHE and citizenship coordinators and youth workers. It is particularly concerned with sex and relationships education (SRE) and with alcohol education.

Blake, S (2001) *Sex and Relationships Education Modules*.
Award Scheme Development Accreditation Network (ASDAN)

This resource pack consists of a range of activities for students, grouped into modules, which concentrate on sex and relationships education within the PSHE/Citizenship areas of the curriculum. Each module consists of a series of challenges or activities for students and a set of suggestions for teachers. The modules are: sex and relationships; staying healthy and safe; people and sex; and understanding more about sex and relationships. The pack consists of 'guidance notes for tutors', together with photocopiable masters of the 'challenge' sheets for pupils, and offers an activity explicitly addressing risk-taking and alcohol use.

Fraser, J (2000) *Drunk in Charge of a Body*. Brook/Alcohol Concern

A teaching pack for use in schools and youth groups aimed at young people aged 13 and over. It facilitates discussion and participatory learning about alcohol and personal and sexual relationships, and increases awareness of the positive and negative influences of alcohol. Cultural values and attitudes, conflict resolution, the development of skills in decision-making, and communication assertiveness are also addressed within the context of alcohol and personal relationships.

Blake, S and Orpin, L (2003) *Sex and Relationships for 14–16 year olds*. CD-ROM and Teachers Manual. Sense Interactive CDs

The CD-ROM provides a scenario about alcohol and sex. This is further developed in the teaching pack. *Sex and relationships education*, a CD-ROM designed to support the DfES guidance on SRE, and the Teenage Pregnancy Strategy. The CD-ROM is accompanied either by a comprehensive teacher's manual or by a short booklet for parents and carers. The teacher's manual provides advice on how to develop a whole-school approach to PSHE as well as ideas on how to use the resource.

Lee, H (2003) *Sex, Drugs and Alcohol*. Tacade

Tacade consulted a wide range of young people during the development of the *Sex, Drugs and Alcohol* education materials published in 2003. These materials are designed for young people aged 14 to 19 of all abilities including those with poor literacy skills.

NCB (2004) *Sex, alcohol and other drugs: Exploring the links* Spotlight Briefing

This briefing highlights the implications for policy and practice from NCB's project Sex, Alcohol and Other Drugs. It offers recommendations for how to improve policy and practice.

Useful organisations

Alcohol Concern
Waterbridge House, 32–36 Loman Street, London SE1 0EE
020 7928 7377
www.alcoholconcern.org.uk
Alcohol Concern is the national agency on alcohol misuse. They work
to reduce the incidence and costs of alcohol-related harm and to
increase the range and quality of services available to people with
alcohol-related problems.

AVERT
4 Brighton Road, Horsham, West Sussex RH13 5BA
01403 210 202
www.avert.org
AVERT is an international HIV and AIDS charity based in the UK, with
the aim of AVERTing HIV and AIDS worldwide. Offers a range of
publications and factsheets on their website.

Black Health Agency
Zion Community Health and Resource Centre, 339 Stretford Road,
Hulme, Manchester M15 4ZY
0161 226 9145
www.blackhealthagency.org.uk
Provides a range of health-related services and initiatives for the
diverse black communities locally, regionally and nationally.

Brook
Unit 421, Highgate Studios, 52–79 Highgate Road, London NW5 1TL
020 7284 6040
Helpline 0800 0185 023 Monday to Friday, 9 am to 5 pm
www.brook.org.uk

Centre for HIV and Sexual Health
22 Collegiate Crescent, Sheffield S10 2BA
0114 226 1900
www.sheffhiv.demon.co.uk
Offers training, consultancy and resources for children, young people
and professionals.

Drug Education Forum
c/o Mentor UK, 4th Floor, 74 Great Eastern Street, London EC2A 3JG
020 7739 8494
www.drugeducation.org.uk
The Drug Education Forum brings together a range of national
organisations from health, education, police and voluntary sectors that
support the delivery of drug education. The Forum promotes the
provision of effective drug education for all children and young people.
The Drug Education Forum believes that the purpose of drug
education is to increase children's and young people's knowledge and
understanding of drugs and their usage, and help them develop skills
and attitudes, so that they can make informed choices.

DrugScope
Waterbridge House, 32–36 Loman Street, London SE1 0EE
020 7928 1211
www.drugscope.org.uk
DrugScope is the UK's leading independent centre of expertise on
drugs. Their aim is to inform policy development and reduce drug-
related risk. They provide quality drug information, promote effective
responses to drug-taking, undertake research at local, national and
international levels, advise on policy-making, encourage informed
debate and speak for its member organisations working on the ground.
24-hour drug helpline 0800 77 66 00.

fpa
2–12 Pentonville Road, London N1 9FP
020 7837 5432
www.fpa.org.uk
Offers training and consultancy as well as resources for children,
young people and professionals. Also runs a helpline: Sexual Health
Direct 0845 310 1334 Monday to Friday, 9 am to 7.30 pm

Health Development Agency
Holborn Gate, 330 High Holborn, London WC1V 7BA
020 7430 0850
www.hda-online.org.uk
Offers research, support and resources. The National HIV Prevention
Information is based at the HDA Service
http://www.hda-online.org.uk/html/nhpis/

Health Initiatives for Youth (HIFY-UK)
Working in Partnership with the UK Coalition, 250 Kennington Lane,
London SE11 5RD
020 7564 2180
Helpline 0800 298 3099
www.hify-uk.com
The only charity of its kind in the UK providing support to young
people living with HIV, educational workshops and supporting clinical
services through peer education. Campaigns for young people's rights
and works with policy and government initiatives.

Image in Action
Chinnor Road, Bledlow Bridge, High Wycombe HP14 4AJ
01494 481 632
Image in Action works with young people with learning disabilities
using drama, group work and active learning to teach sex education.

National Children's Bureau
8 Wakley Street, London EC1V 7QE
020 7843 6000
www.ncb.org.uk
Offers an information service and produces a range of resources
including a (currently) free termly newsletter, *Spotlight: Promoting
emotional, social development* (to order a copy email
spotlight@ncb.org.uk), and offers training and consultancy on all
aspects of PSHE and Citizenship.

National Healthy School Standard
Holborn Gate, 330 High Holborn, London WC1V 7BA
020 7061 3072
www.wiredforhealth.gov.uk
The National team provides support and advice to local health and
education partnerships.

NAZ Project London
Palingswick House, 241 King Street, London W6 9LP
020 8741 1879
NAZ Project London (NPL) provides sexual health and HIV prevention
and support services to the South Asian, Middle Eastern, North
African, Horn of African and Latin American communities in London as
well as resources.

Parent to Parent
C/O Centre for HIV and Sexual Health, 22 Collegiate Crescent,
Sheffield S10 2BA
0114 226 1917

Parentline Plus
520 Highgate Studios, 53–79 Highgate Road, London NW5 1TL
www.parentlineplus.org.uk
Free helpline 0808 800 2222
Confidential 24-hour service for anyone looking after a child – parent,
step-parent, grandparent, step-grandparent, or foster carer.

Qualifications and Curriculum Authority
83 Piccadilly, London W1J 8QA
020 7509 5555
Lines are open Monday–Friday 8.30 am to 5.30 pm
Enquiry line: 020 7509 5556
Lines are open Monday–Friday 9 am to 5 pm
Minicom: 020 7509 6546
www.qca.org.uk
The QCA provides guidance on PSHE and schemes of work on drugs
including alcohol and tobacco.

Relate
Herbert Gray College, Little Church Street, Rugby, Warwickshire CV21 3AP
0845 456 1310 or 01788 573241
www.relate.org.uk
Relationship Education and Training Department provides training for
professionals in SRE.

Sex Education Forum
8 Wakley Street, London EC1V 7QE
020 7843 1901
www.ncb.org.uk/sef
The Sex Education Forum is the national authority on sex and
relationships education (SRE). The Forum believes that good quality
SRE is an entitlement for all children and young people. We
are working with our 49 member organisations to achieve this.
SEF publishes a range of factsheets and publications.

Tacade
Old Exchange Building, 6 St Ann's Passage, King Street, Manchester
M2 6AD
0161 836 6859
Email: info@tacade.co.uk
www.tacade.com
The Teachers' Advisory Council on Alcohol and Drugs Education
(TACADE) is a charitable organisation that provides a range of
publications, training and consultancy products and services for those
working with young people.

Terence Higgins Trust
52–54 Grays Inn Road, London WC1X 8JU
020 7831 0330
www.tht.org.uk
THT is the leading HIV and AIDS charity in the UK and the largest in
Europe. It offers a helpline as well as training and resources.

Working with Men
320 Commercial Way, London SE15 1QN
020 8308 0709
Provides training and resources for working with boys and young men.

References

Adams, J (1997) *Girlpower – how far does it go? A resource and training pack on girls, young women and self-esteem*. Centre for HIV and Sexual Health

Adams, J (2002) *Go Girls! Supporting emotional development and self-esteem*. Centre for HIV and Sexual Health

Aggleton, P *et al*. (1998) *Reducing the rates of teenage conceptions: The implications of research into young people, sex, sexuality and relationships*. Health Education Authority

Alcohol Concern (2002) *Alcohol and Teenage Pregnancy*

AXM (August 2003) *Escape the Rat Race*

Ball, D (2002) *Playgrounds: Risks, benefits and choices*. Middlesex University, Sudbury. HSE Books

Beinhart, S *et al*. (2002) *A National Survey of Problem Behaviour and Associated Risk and Protective Factors among Young People*. Joseph Rowntree Foundation

Biddulph, M and Blake, S (2001) *Moving goalposts: Setting a training agenda for sexual health work with boys and young men*. fpa

Blake, S (2003) *Young Gay Men Talking: Issues and Ideas for Action*. Working with Men

Blake, S and Lynch, J (2004 forthcoming) *Sex and Relationships Education in Pupil Referral Units*. Sex Education Forum

Brook and Alcohol Concern (2001) *Drunk in Charge of a Body*. Brook and Alcohol Concern

Brown, H and Craft, A (1992) *Working with the Unthinkable*. Family Planning Association

Coleman, L (2001) 'Young People, Risk and Sexual Behaviour: A Literature Review'. HDA (unpublished)

Corlyon, J and McGuire, C (1997) *Young Parents in Public Care: Pregnancy and Parenthood among Young People looked after by Local Authorities*. National Children's Bureau

Dennison, C and Coleman, J (2002) *Young People and Gender – a Review of Research*. Women's Unit

Department for Education and Skills (2003a) *Drugs: Guidance for Schools Consultation Document*

Department for Education and Skills (2003b) *Every Child Matters*

Department of Health (2003) *Statistics on young people and drug misuse: England, 2002.*

Department of Health/DrugScope (2002) *Taking Care with Drugs: Responding to Substance Misuse amongst Looked After Children*. DrugScope

Elliot, K J and Lambourne, A J (1999) 'Sex, Drugs and Alcohol: two peer-led approaches in Tamaki Makaurau/Auckland, New Zealand', *Journal of Adolescence*, 22, 4, 503–13

Giddens, A (1991) *Modernity and Self-identity: Self and Society in the Late Modern Age.* Polity Press

Gilvarry, E *(ed.)* (2001) *The substance of young needs review 2001.* Health Advisory Service

Hayes, M (2002) *Taking Chances: The Lifestyles and Leisure Risk of Young People.* Child Accident Prevention Trust

Health Development Agency (2003) *Teenage pregnancy and parenthood: a review of reviews*

Henderson, S (1997) *Ecstasy: Case Unsolved.* Pandora

Henderson, S (2002) *Protection and It's a Fine Line: An evaluation of two multi component interventions targeting drug use and sexual health in the context of nightlife in Merseyside and Ibiza.* HIT

Hibell, B *et al.* (2001) *The 1999 ESPAD report: Alcohol and Other Drug Use amongst Students in 30 European Countries.* Stockholm: Swedish Council for Information on alcohol and other drugs

Hingson, R W *et al.* (1990) 'Beliefs about AIDS, use of alcohol and drugs, and unprotected sex among Massachusetts adolescents', *American Journal of Public* Health, 80, 295–9

Ingham, R (2001) 'Young People, Alcohol and Sexual Conduct', *Sex Education Matters*, No. 27, 9–10

Ingham, R, Woodcock, A and Stenner, K (1991) *Getting to know you ... young people's knowledge of their partners at first intercourse,* Journal of Community and Applied Social Psychology, 1, 2, 117–32

Lee, H (2003) *Sex, Drugs and Alcohol – for young people aged 14–19 with a range of abilities.* Tacade

Leigh, B (1999) 'Peril, chance, adventure: concepts of risk, alcohol use and risky behaviour in young adults', *Addiction*, 94, 371–83.

Lloyd, T (2002) 'Young Men, Risk Taking and Health'. Unpublished paper prepared for the SADLE Project. Sex Education Forum and Drug Education Forum

MacHale, E and Newell, J (1997) 'Sexual behaviour and sex education in Irish school-going teenagers', *International Journal of STD and AIDS*, 8, 196–200

Mason, A and Palmer, A (1995) *'Queer Bashing – a survey of hate crimes against gay men and lesbians.* Stonewall

McGrellis, S *et al.* (2000) *Through the Moral Maze: a quantitative study of young people's values.* The Tufnell Press

National Children's Bureau (2003) *A whole school approach to PSHE and Citizenship*

National Healthy School Standard (2004 forthcoming) *Supporting Pupil Participation*

Palmer, T (2001) *No Son of Mine! Children Abused through Prostitution.* Report and video. Barnardos

Plant, M and Miller, P (2000) 'Drug use has declined among teenagers in the United Kingdom', *British Medical Journal*, 320, p. 1536

Plant, M, Bagnall, G and Foster, J (1990) 'Teenage Heavy Drinkers: alcohol-related knowledge, beliefs, experiences, motivation and the social context of drinking', *Alcohol and Alcoholism*, 25, 691–8

Qualifications and Curriculum Authority (1999a) *National Curriculum Handbook for Primary Schools*

Qualifications and Curriculum Authority (1999b) *National Curriculum Handbook for Secondary Schools*

Rhodes, T and Quirk, A (1996) *Sexual Safety and Drug Use, London.* Centre for Research on Drugs and Health Behaviour

Santelli, J S, Brener, N D, Lowry, R, Bhatt, A, Zabin, L S (1998) 'Multiple sexual partners among US adolescents and young adults', *Family Planning Perspectives*, 30, 271–81.

Social Exclusion Unit (1999) *Teenage Pregnancy.* HMSO

Van Meeuwen, A, Swann, S *et al.* (1998) *Whose Daughter Next? Children Abused through Prostitution.* Report and video. Barnardos

Wellings, K *et al.* (1994) National Survey of Sexual Attitudes and Lifestyles.

Wright, D, Henderson, M, Rabb, G. *et al.* (2000) 'Extent of regretted sexual intercourse among young teenagers in Scotland: a cross sectional survey' *British Medical Journal*, vol 320, 12, 433–44

www.ingramcontent.com/pod-product-compliance
Ingram Content Group UK Ltd.
Pitfield, Milton Keynes, MK11 3LW, UK
UKHW051900270225
455659UK00014B/131